JOURNAL OF MORAL THEOLOGY

VOLUME 8, SPECIAL ISSUE NUMBER 1
SPRING 2019

CONTINGENT FACULTY

Edited by
Matthew J. Gaudet
James F. Keenan. S.J.

JOURNAL · OF
M · O · R · A · L
THEOLOGY

Journal of Moral Theology is published semiannually, with regular issues in January and June. Our mission is to publish scholarly articles in the field of Catholic moral theology, as well as theological treatments of related topics in philosophy, economics, political philosophy, and psychology.

Articles published in the *Journal of Moral Theology* undergo at least two double blind peer reviews. Authors are asked to submit articles electronically to jmt@msmary.edu. Submissions should be prepared for blind review. Microsoft Word format preferred. The editors assume that submissions are not being simultaneously considered for publication in another venue.

Journal of Moral Theology is available full text in the *ATLA Religion Database with ATLASerials®* (RDB®), a product of the American Theological Library Association.
Email: atla@atla.com, www: http://www.atla.com.
ISSN 2166-2851 (print)
ISSN 2166-2118 (online)

Journal of Moral Theology is published by Mount St. Mary's University, 16300 Old Emmitsburg Road, Emmitsburg, MD 21727.

Copyright© 2019 individual authors and Mount St. Mary's University. All rights reserved.

Except for brief quotations in critical publications or reviews, no part of this book may be reproduced in any manner without prior written permission from the publisher. Write: Permissions. Wipf and Stock Publishers, 199 W. 8th Ave., Suite 3, Eugene, OR 97401.

Pickwick Publications, An Imprint of Wipf and Stock Publishers, 199 W. 8th Ave., Suite 3, Eugene, OR 97401. www.wipfandstock.com. ISBN 13: 978-1-5326-8674-0

JOURNAL · OF
M · O · R · A · L
THEOLOGY

EDITOR EMERITUS AND UNIVERSITY LIAISON
David M. McCarthy, *Mount St. Mary's University*

EDITOR
Jason King, *Saint Vincent College*

SENIOR EDITOR
William J. Collinge, *Mount St. Mary's University*

ASSOCIATE EDITOR
M. Therese Lysaught, *Loyola University Chicago*

MANAGING EDITOR
Kathy Criasia, *Mount St. Mary's University*

BOOK REVIEW EDITORS
Kent Lasnoski, *Quincy University*
Christopher McMahon, *Saint Vincent College*

EDITORIAL BOARD
Jana M. Bennett, *University of Dayton*
Mara Brecht, *St. Norbert College*
Jim Caccamo, *St. Joseph's University*
Meghan Clark, *St. John's University*
David Cloutier, *The Catholic University of America*
Christopher Denny, *St. John's University*
Matthew Gaudet, *Santa Clara University*
Mari Rapela Heidt, *Waukesha, Wisconsin*
Kelly Johnson, *University of Dayton*
Andrew Kim, *Marquette University*
Warren Kinghorn, *Duke University*
John Love, *Mount St. Mary's Seminary*
Ramon Luzarraga, *Benedictine University, Mesa*
William C. Mattison III, *University of Notre Dame*
Christopher McMahon, *Saint Vincent College*
Mary M. Doyle Roche, *College of the Holy Cross*
Joel Shuman, *Kings College*
Matthew Shadle, *Marymount University*
Christopher P. Vogt, *St. John's University*
Brian Volck, *University of Cincinnati College of Medicine*
Paul Wadell, *St. Norbert College*
Greg Zuschlag, *Oblate School of Theology*

Journal of Moral Theology
Volume 8, Special Issue Number 1
Spring 2019

Contents

Introduction
  Matthew J. Gaudet and James F. Keenan, S.J. 1

University Ethics and Contingent Faculty
  James F. Keenan, S.J. 8

Saying No to an Economy that Kills: Undermining Mission and Exploiting Vocation in Catholic Higher Education
  Kerry Danner 26

Adjunct Unionization on Catholic Campuses: Solidarity, Theology, and Mission
  Debra Erickson 51

The Threat to Academic Freedom and the Contingent Scholar
  Lincoln R. Rice 75

Contingency, Gender, and the Academic Table
  Karen Peterson-Iyer 92

The Spiritual Crisis of Contingent Faculty
  Claire Bischoff 115

Departmental Chair as Faculty Advocate and Middle Manager
  Elizabeth Hinson-Hasty 126

Toward an Inclusive Faculty Community
  Matthew J. Gaudet 141

Contributors 160

Introduction

Matthew J. Gaudet and James F. Keenan, S.J.

TODAY OVER 70 PERCENT OF COLLEGE faculty in America work off of the tenure-track on some kind of fixed-term contract. Their service might be for a term, a year, or, rarely, multiple years, but even the longest of these is typically revocable at the discretion of the university and wholly dependent of the needs of the university. At some schools, it is common practice for contracts to be revoked even after the term has begun, as course enrollments are ironed out and the final needs of the school are accounted for. In short, to be a contingent professor is to risk losing one's livelihood at any moment.

At the same time, the university business model today is deeply reliant on contingent faculty labor. Not only do short and revocable contracts allow universities to provide students with "just in time" scheduling with little risk to the institution, but the low pay and lack of benefits that typically go with contingent contracts are deeply embedded in the economics of how most colleges and universities operate today. Many schools would have difficulties remaining fiscally solvent without contingent labor as we know it.

In the end, efforts to replace or even modify the unjust system would require a wholesale restructuring of the enterprise of higher education as we know it. Currently, there is little will among the powers-that-be to take up such a restructuring. Our highest aspiration in putting this volume together is that these essays might do their part to bring about such wholesale change. More modestly, we at least hope the articles presented here open a space for greater scholarly conversation about the role of non-tenure track faculty on Catholic (and all) college campuses for, despite a growing audience for scholarly work on the ethics of contingency work, prior to the publication of this issue there had not been a good outlet for such scholarship.

We found this out the hard way. The origins of this issue of the *Journal of Moral Theology* (JMT) can be traced to the 2017 Annual Meeting of the Society of Christian Ethics (SCE) in New Orleans. At that meeting, the SCE Caucus for Contingent Faculty Concerns (CCFC) had organized a panel of contingent scholars to respond to James Keenan, S.J.'s then newly published book *University Ethics:*

How Colleges Can Build and Benefit from a Culture of Ethics. Debra Erickson and Lincoln Rice had organized and were convening the discussion, Matthew Gaudet and Karen Peterson-Iyer were two of the three panelists, and Keenan was to respond to the panel. Several other authors in this volume were also in attendance at the session, as was Jason King, the editor of the *Journal of Moral Theology*. The session was well received by all who attended, and the subsequent discussion was intelligent, constructive, and, groundbreaking in the sense that it was the first sustained and academic discussion of contingency at the SCE. From here, however, the story diverged into two tracks. On the one hand, conversation regarding contingency was burgeoning throughout the broader theological academy, especially at the SCE and the American Academy of Religion (AAR). On the other, there did not seem to be any place for *scholarship* on ethics and contingency.

Following a successful advocacy campaign by several contingent faculty in its membership, the American Academy of Religion had commissioned a Contingent Faculty Task Force in 2014, charged to examine "issues of contingency labor in religious studies as well as to advocate for contingent faculty and make recommendations to the AAR to address the needs of contingent academic labor in religious studies."[1] In 2015, AAR began offering travel grants for contingent faculty to attend the annual meeting, and, in 2016, when the Task Force completed its work, the board of the AAR replaced it with a permanent working group aimed at contingency as well as a "Contingent Faculty Director" position on the AAR Board. Kerry Danner would be elected co-chair of the working group in 2016 and then elected as the first Contingent Faculty Director in 2017. In 2018, the AAR added access to JSTOR's religion and theology collection as a member benefit, with an aim to stem one of the impacts of contingent contracts being cancelled or not renewed.

Back at the SCE, Karen Peterson-Iyer had been elected to the Board of the SCE in 2014 and, to this day, remains the only contingent scholar to serve in that capacity. Her voice on the Board, combined with skillful advocacy by CCFC co-conveners Debra Erickson and Lincoln Rice, began to open eyes to the plight of the contingent scholar in our midst, the moral issues involved, and the effects this sea change might have on the very notion of a scholarly society. In 2015,

---

[1] The open letter that is given credit for catalyzing for AAR's response to contingency was Kate Daley-Bailey's "For the Good of the Guild: An Open Letter to the American Academy of Religion." Daley-Bailey would later acknowledge her letter was informed, in part, by a prior letter written by Debra Erickson, in response to an AAR decision to adjust one of the hotels for their 2011 annual meeting because the hotel was in an ongoing labor dispute. Erickson questioned why the same solidarity was not being afforded to the blighted workers *within* the academy.

the SCE Board had commissioned a Professional Development committee to find ways to better serve those in transition from doctoral programs to employment, both professorial and otherwise. Meanwhile, the Caucus for Contingent Faculty Concerns was strongly encouraged by all in attendance at the New Orleans session to continue to sponsor panels for discussion at the SCE Annual Meeting. Thus, in 2018, the CCFC invited Jason King and Elizabeth Hinson-Hasty to reflect on contingency from their perspective as department heads, with Danner serving as respondent, offering her view as both contingent scholar and advocate.

In 2017-18, David Gushee would rise to be both President of the SCE and President-Elect of the AAR. Following conversations about contingency in both organizations, Gushee became "more sensitized to the increasingly dark labor market problems and began to see that these were ethical issues—and also vocational issues, collegiality issues, and more"[2] He had also decided to dedicate his presidential year at the SCE to underrepresented voices. Thus, he invited the CCFC to host the 2018 SCE Forum, a preconference event in which participants took up a topic of interest to the whole SCE in a plenary session before the main conference began. The team that designed, presented, and led the Forum included Rice, Erickson, Danner, Peterson-Iyer, and Gaudet. Also in 2018, the SCE Board commissioned its own Task Force on Contingency, co-chaired by Gaudet and including Keenan, Peterson-Iyer, and Danner as members. At the publication of this issue, the work of that Task Force is still ongoing.

Despite the successful advocacy work and ever-expanding conversation on the topic at AAR, SCE, and other scholarly societies, there still did not seem to be a place for thoughtful Christian ethicists to take up the morality of academic contingency as a *scholarly* topic. The papers of the New Orleans panel were submitted for publication to numerous journals. They were offered both as a joint-authored paper by all of the panelists, including Keenan's response, and as individual stand-alone essays. They were also submitted to other journals in several different disciplines, including education and Christian theology. Despite these efforts, none of the papers submitted were accepted for publication. More importantly, the general response, from all disciplines was the same: "this is interesting work, but it just does not fit with we do here at XXX journal."

Frustrated by the lack of space for scholarly conversation on ethics and contingency but buoyed by the growing interest in the subject, in the summer of 2017, we finally turned to the editor of *JMT*, Jason King. He responded almost immediately and offered to run a special

---

[2] Email exchange between Matthew Gaudet and David Gushee, August 14, 2018.

issue of the *JMT* to get the topic to press as soon as possible.[3] Thus, the *JMT* special issue on Contingency at Catholic Colleges was born, and there was finally a place for sustained theological and scholarly work on contingency.

We offer this history to the reader for three reasons. First, you will notice a significant overlap between the names mentioned in this narrative and the editor and author list for this issue. That is neither coincidental nor accidental. Several of the articles in this issue have their roots in the panels named above and the versions here are the product of a continuing conversation these authors have been having for many years. Also, several of the late drafts were shared with other authors in the volume to help cross-fertilize the ideas. As a result, this issue has a maturity to it, not just in the essays that have been developed over time but also in how they coalesce with each other. Our hope is that, in turn, the conversations here prompt wider and further discussion throughout the academy.

Secondly, it is worth acknowledging that those who strive for academic worker justice are both advocates and scholars. Thus, the essays in this volume are unmistakably informed by personal experience but raised to a scholarly level and placed into necessary conversation with Catholic social teaching as well as Catholic ideas of mission, vocation, and higher education itself.

The final reason we offer the history above is that it informs the structure of the issue itself. The overarching goal of this volume is to attend to the reality of contingency today in light of pertinent Catholic teachings on education, social structures, and economic justice. The essays in this volume will proceed in three parts. Part I is a single essay offered by Keenan that situates the issue of contingency within the broader field of university ethics. The original New Orleans panel responded to Keenan's text *University Ethics* and much of what is done in these pages is owed to that antecedent.[4] In his opening essay of this text, Keenan offers an expanded version of his thoughts on the issue of contingency, including insights, claims, and observations that he has continued to develop since *University Ethics* was published.

The task of Part II is to examine the intricate details and facets of the main subject. To this end, the five authors in this section each offer a snapshot of one of the most glaring concerns regarding contingency today as well as suggestions for solutions to address these acute concerns. The selection of these particular snapshots was not accidental but rather the result of careful and collaborative work by the interlocutors to take up several different perspectives on the same subject so as to leave the listener with a thick, multi-dimensional image of the

---

[3] Email exchange between Matthew Gaudet and Jason King, July 3, 2017.
[4] Seven of the eight essays in this issue either quote or cite *University Ethics*.

subject. The first four essays of part II all have their roots in the "SCE Forum" that occurred before the 2018 SCE Annual Meeting. A team of six scholars planned that event over the course of several months and five of those six—Kerry Danner, Debra Erickson, Lincoln Rice, Karen Peterson-Iyer and Matthew Gaudet—are represented in these pages.[5] Offered a blank slate to present the complex issues of contingency to an entire academic society, this team spent months discussing and parsing the questions of contingency in order to develop a program that was both comprehensive and accessible.

First, Kerry Danner sets the stage by exploring recent but significant shifts in the economic structures of academic life and the relationship of these shifting structures to Catholic social thought, the mission of Catholic higher education, and the vocation of the professor at Catholic schools. She then offers some concrete suggestions for how to move forward with an eye to economic justice and Catholic morality.

Debra Erickson follows Danner with an examination of the role of faculty unions at Catholic colleges. Using recent trends and specific cases, Erickson plots the range of recent responses to unionization by the administrators of several Catholic colleges and challenges those Catholic schools who have sought to thwart unionization as not only not in keeping with Catholic Social Teaching on worker justice but also in violation of the Catholic notion of the university.

Next, Lincoln Rice shifts our attention to individual rights and, specifically, a right to the protections of tenure for contingent faculty. Making a strong case that such protections are as necessary for quality teaching as they are for quality research, Rice argues in favor of universal tenure, even if the contemporary university continues to hire faculty into non-research teaching roles.

Karen Peterson-Iyer then addresses the "gradual but distinct feminization of contingent labor in institutions of higher education." Engaging a wide range of Christian and non-Christian feminist authors, Peterson-Iyer paints a vivid picture of both the root causes and the effects of a system in which women consistently earn at least half of all Ph.Ds. but are nevertheless 10-15 percent more likely than their male peers to hold contingent roles.

Finally, Claire Bischoff offers a compelling argument that contingent work is the cause of a *spiritual* crisis for both individual contingent faculty and the institutions they serve. Framing her essay around

---

[5] Many thanks are offered to the sixth member of that team, Darrin Snyder-Belousek of Ohio Northern University. Though Darrin did not include an essay for this volume, he is no doubt represented in the other five essays that emerged from this thoughtful and reflective planning team.

Thea Bowman's notion of spirituality as self-awareness, other-awareness, and God-awareness, Bischoff shows how contingency interferes with each of these interior sensibilities and in turn, harms our ability to be great institutions of education and learning.[6]

Taken individually, Danner, Erickson, Rice, Peterson-Iyer, and Bischoff each offer the reader a detailed and nuanced examination of the thorniest moral questions within the topic of contingency. Collectively, however, they capture a rich, layered, and multi-dimensional image of the plight of the contingent professor, which is unrivaled in the literature on the subject to date.

Having laid this foundation, Part III redirects attention once more, from the subject (the contingent scholar) to the observer of the picture (the reader). Part III of the volume pivots away from acute issues and towards those who will need to respond to these issues. First, Hinson-Hasty offers a view from the seat of (marginal) power, as she wrestles with the limits and responsibilities of tenured faculty and, in particular, department chairs in the contemporary university structure. Seeking to "reflect authentically and honestly out of [her] own experience about the cognitive dissonance and moral incoherence one encounters when navigating two worlds—the world of tenured faculty and the world of contingency"—Hinson-Hasty acknowledges the limits that one has as a "middle manager" in academia but nevertheless challenges her fellow department heads and senior faculty members to "envision alternatives and affect the current consumer-driven trajectory of higher education."

Finally, in the coda essay of the volume, Gaudet offers a bookend to match Keenan's opening essay. Where Keenan's essay begins with consideration of the university as a whole (and its lack of ethically driven culture) but narrows the focus to contingency, Gaudet widens the aperture, keeping contingency as the subject, but also bringing the wider university community back into clear view. Looking toward a brighter future for contingent scholars, Gaudet first clears the way by debunking several of the myths which sustain the current divided and individualistic university culture. Then, drawing upon both Catholic Social thought and direct appeals to scripture, he calls the entire institution of Catholic higher education to a recommitment to solidarity

---

[6] It is worth noting that Bischoff is the only author in Part II who was not part of the SCE Forum team. (Her essay was first presented at the 2018 College Theology Society annual meeting, for which Jason King served as convener.) She is also the only scholar in this volume who is not an ethicist by training and scholarship. The relationship between those two facts is not incidental. As ethicists we all-too-often overlook the spiritual effects of the issues we take up. (This was the case in the SCE Forum on Contingency.) Nevertheless, Bischoff does a fine job of reminding us of the necessary connections between the spiritual and the moral, especially when it comes to the present topic.

and the common good as we collectively work towards a better and more inclusive university community.

This volume is intended to fill lacunae in the fields of Christian ethics and higher education studies. Prior to this volume, there were a few scattered scholarly pieces on Christian ethics and academic contingency, but the vast majority of work done on the topic limited to journalism and advocacy. Our hope is that this volume both engenders further conversation on the ethics of contingency and becomes the scholarly foundation of many future conversations. ∎

University Ethics and Contingent Faculty

James F. Keenan, S.J.

IN THIS ESSAY, I connect the issue of university ethics to that of contingent faculty. I share my own experience of encounter with institutional ethics by referring to the issues of the church that I found as a priest and as an ethicist while living in Boston during the sex abuse scandal. The lessons I learned there helped me to turn to the other institution that teaches ethics, the university, that like the church (until recently) has little institutional interest or engagement in sustaining a culture of institutional accountability. Then, I raise the issue of contemporary scandals as prompting "interruptions" in university life that suggest that, like the church, it too needs to promote a culture of ethics. To highlight how deep and problematic the university landscape is without a culture of ethics, I offer one example by addressing the issue of "interests in race" on the contemporary campus. I propose two strategic obstacles that impede developing such a culture on campus: the "individualistic" vocation of the faculty member and what I call the "geography" of the American university. I present some of the ethical issues that connect to contingency, especially highlighting how these obstacles further aggravate the ethical issues around contingency. I conclude with a call for the hermeneutics of professional ethics as constitutive for university flourishment.

LESSONS FROM THE PEWS

One of the first lessons from the sex abuse scandals that rocked the churches, and in particular, the Roman Catholic Church, is that, though the churches taught ethics to its parishioners, it instructed neither its administrators nor its clergy and lay ministers in any professional ethics. Though it taught ethics to the pews, it did not practice it in the rectories because it did not believe that it needed ethics. It presumed if it could teach ethics, it did not need them.

Before the scandals interrupted its life, the church had neither stipulated its commitment to ethics nor developed the infrastructure to engage its own ethical accountability. Like the academy today, the church had no internal culture of professional ethical transparency. By looking at the church, therefore, we might understand the university's situation all the better.

During the sex abuse crisis, the absence of a culture of ethics in the church has become repeatedly evident. Ethics was not only lacking among the predatory priests but was also noticeably absent in the decision-making by bishops and their counselors as they transferred such priests, failed to notify civil authorities, stonewalled and defamed the reputations of concerned and aggrieved parents, and left children at profound risk.

Ethics was also not evident even after the harm was done. As the crisis unfolded, innocent priests were not protected, due process was often breached, financial mismanagement frequently occurred, lay initiatives were treated with scorn, derision, and suspicion, and priests who protested episcopal mismanagement were targeted.[1]

Why was ethics so absent? Why did anyone in clerical or episcopal life so rarely ask of their decisions and their practices the simple question, "is this ethical?" Did they have the language, structure and practices to even ask, let alone answer, the question, "But is this ethical?"

Unlike many other professions, religious leaders rarely turned to ethical norms to consider what constitutes right conduct in their field of leadership and service. I do not mean by this that religious leaders or their decisions were or are unethical. Rather, I mean that when religious, clergy and bishops exercised routine decision-making they turned to a multitude of considerations, but articulated ethical norms, their specific values, virtues and goods, and the type of critical thinking that estimates the long-standing social claims that these values, goods and virtues have on us were not and still are not explicitly, professionally engaged. In a word, ethical norms, critical ethical reasoning, and attendant ethical practices, which frequently aid other professionals in law, business, medicine, counseling, nursing, engineering, and even politics, played a much less explicit role in ecclesial leadership practices. This question, "But is it ethical?" was absent in the churches not only in matters about sexual boundaries but also in matters about financial responsibility, personal and social accountability,

---

[1] James F. Keenan and Joseph J. Kotva, Jr., ed., *Practice What You Preach: Virtues, Ethics and Power in the Lives of Pastoral Ministers and Their Congregations* (Lanham: Sheed and Ward, 1999); James F. Keenan, *Practice What You Preach: The Need For Ethics in Church Leadership (*Annual Jesuit Lecture in Human Values*)* (Milwaukee: Center for Ethics Studies, Marquette University, 2000); "Toward an Ecclesial Professional Ethics," in *Church Ethics and its Organizational Context: Learning from the Sex Abuse Scandal in the Catholic Church*, ed. Jean Bartunek, Mary Ann Hinsdale, and James Keenan (Lanham: Sheed and Ward, 2005), 83-96; "Church Leadership, Ethics, and the Moral Rights of Priests," in *Moral Theology for the Twenty-First Century: Essays in Honor of Kevin Kelly*, ed. Bernard Hoose, Julie Clague, and Gerard Mannion (London: T and T Clark, 2008), 204-219.

the claims of confidentiality, the importance of truth-telling, due process, consultation, contracts, fair wages, adequate representation, appeals, and conflicts of interests.

Creating and supporting a culture of professional ethical discourse, mandating ethical training, and requiring ethical accountability ought not to be seen as inimical to the interests of the church or its mission but rather constitutive of it. Today, as the church continues to emerge from its scandals, it is only beginning to learn that the professional ethics of its ministers and other employees do not inhibit or compromise the mission of the church but rather supports its credibility, its community building activity, and its teaching and realization of the truth. In *The Origins of Christian Morality*, Wayne Meeks stated simply, "Making morals means making community."[2] This insight runs throughout this essay because promoting the issue of professional ethics does not and will not inhibit or compromise the work of the university. Rather, it promotes institutional flourishing.

UNIVERSITIES INTERRUPTED BY SCANDALS

Ten years ago, I began noticing a second set of institutional scandals in the newspapers, those at universities and colleges. In time, I began combing newspapers to see how often these scandals were being reported. What I found were many scandals, but not anyone calling them ethical ones. Our universities were riddled with ethical compromise, but rarely, even when the press exposed something scandalous or shameful about a university, did we identify the issue as a lack of ethics.

Still, every day, I find something problematic at a university: it could be about an athlete, an advancement scheme, a student suicide, a campus sexual assault, a cheating scandal, a trustee member's conflict of interest, or an adjunct faculty member's poor treatment. Every day, I could find something that suggested that university ethical scandals were a commonplace: the cheating scandal at Harvard; athletic/academic fraud at the University of North Carolina; the rape allegations at the University of Virginia; the settlement at University of Colorado over the dismissal of a faculty member; the hazing death at Florida A&M University; the firing of the President and football coach at Penn State in light of sexual misconduct; the pepper-spraying of students at the University of California at Davis, etc., etc., etc.

I began wondering: Are these issues sensational but isolated moments across the academic landscape or is there something more systemic here? I came to believe it was systemic. In other forms of professional life, we have long recognized a strong connection between

---

[2] Wayne Meeks, *The Origins of Christian Morality* (New Haven: Yale University Press, 1995), 5.

the lack of a professional ethics in a particular institutional setting and the lack of an ethical consciousness in that culture. I believe that the absence of a professional ethics at the university is evidence of and symptomatic of a university culture disinterested in ethics. Simply put, our universities do not believe that they *need* ethics. Like the church, they seem to sense that if they can teach ethics, they don't need them.

Still, this is odd. At any university, anyone can take a course on business ethics, nursing ethics, legal ethics, medical ethics, or journalistic ethics. Ethics courses in the different professions are easily available at almost any university. In fact, generally speaking, if one is looking for ethical training in any profession, the courses are found only at a university. The one major professional institution about which you cannot find any ethics courses listed among courses at any university is precisely the university. If you search for a course on university ethics, you will simply not find one.

Though professors and their deans recognize the need to teach professional ethics in all the other professions, they show no real interest in professional ethics for their own. Most of all, the administrators, in particular, those at the highest level of the university, from vice-presidents and the president to the board of trustees, have not been trained in professional university ethics. Small wonder then that they do not promote a culture of ethical consciousness and accountability.

None of us throughout the academy are really trained to be ethical in the standards we use for grading papers, for seeing students, for maintaining office hours, for evaluating colleagues or prospective hires. We have not been taught anything about professional confidentiality, boundaries with our students, writing evaluative letters for or about others, or about keeping our contracts. We have not addressed the fact that our salaries are disproportionate or that tenure decisions sometimes lack "objectivity." We do not have professional questions about our university investments, budgets, or boards of trustees, nor do we review adequately fellow faculty after tenure or after being given endowed chairs. Matters like sustainability on campus, faculty or staff unions, university relations with neighbors, students' rights, sexual health issues, boards of trustees' terms of office, conflict of interest laws, workers' benefits, immigration issues, racial tensions, the dorm life of students, the overemphasis on research and the failure to reward good teaching, or the harm of classism experienced by many students unable to keep up with the costs of education, might occasionally garner an individual faculty member's attention, but for the most part, we leave that to academic administrators who, like the faculty, have no training in ethics.

Let me conclude with one compelling example of the lack of any interest in university ethics: the cataloguing of books on professional ethics in university libraries. When I began this project eight years ago, I investigated my own university library. Then we had over 400,000 books stacked in our library. There each book is assigned a subject heading. Under the subject "medical ethics," we had 1321 books; under "business ethics," 599 books; under "nursing ethics," 234 books; under "legal ethics," 129 books; under "clergy ethics," 25 (relatively new) books; and, under "academic ethics," 5 (brand new) books.

As our library's five newly minted books suggest, the field of academic ethics is struggling to emerge. What are those five new books? Besides my own[3], another one is entitled *The Ethical Challenges of Academic Administrators*. Like mine, the editors begin their introduction noting that their book is "intended as a first word, not the final word on the subject. This is the case," they write, "in part, because the practical activity of academic administration has not been the subject of much sustained ethical reflection."[4] The field is, as you can see, brand new.[5]

Still, this lack of books on academic ethics is alarming inasmuch as academics, more than business people, nurses, doctors and lawyers, develop their careers precisely by writing books! Our métier and promotional mantra is "publish or perish." While we publish books on professional ethics in other fields, we apparently have very little interest in the field of professional university ethics. Concomitantly, just as we do not write books on the topic, we do not teach the courses either. But then, none of us seem to be aware of this.

FOR INSTANCE, RACE AND DIVERSITY ON COLLEGE CAMPUSES

After the election of Donald Trump as president, university campuses seemed to erupt with a variety of conflicts, among them racial ones.[6] One could look at these incidents as simple signs of the times,

---

[3] James F. Keenan, *University Ethics: How Colleges Can Build and Benefit from a Culture of Ethics* (New York: Rowman and Littlefield, 2015).
[4] Elaine E. Englehardt, Michael S. Pritchard, Kerry D. Romesburg, Brian E. Schrag, eds., *The Ethical Challenges of Academic Administration* (New York: Springer, 2010), xiii. They refer to two earlier works, Rudolph Weingartner, *Moral Dimensions of the Academic Administration* (Lanham: Rowman and Littlefield, 1999) and Paul Olscamp, *Moral Leadership and the Presidency* (Lanham: Rowman and Littlefield, 2003).
[5] The term academic ethics has since been largely replaced with university ethics in part because some of the ethical issues related to a university are not actually academic, e.g., sexual assault, binge drinking, and conflict of interest.
[6] Dan Bauman, "After 2016 Election, Campus Hate Crimes Seemed to Jump. Here's What the Data Tell Us," *The Chronicle of Higher Education*, February 16, 2018, www.chronicle.com/article/After-2016-Election-Campus/242577. See also Jane Mayer, "A Conservative Nonprofit That Seeks to Transform College Campuses Faces

but anyone interested in university ethics would ask, were American universities already ethically sensitive to the issues of race on campus? Was there already on the American campus a culture of ethics that promoted racial understanding and the Trump election just unsettled a culture already prepared for racist intrusions? Or was the campus as disinterested in race as in most matters ethical and therefore surprised by the interruption? What did these interruptions reveal?

Unfortunately, the university was as asleep on race as on most ethical issues.[7] In fact, universities actually have a negative impact on racial sensitivity. The longer students are in college, the less interested they become in promoting racial understanding. This was the central finding of a long-term, comprehensive study from six years ago in which students were asked throughout their college years, "How important to you personally is helping to promote racial understanding?" The question was posed to the students upon their arrival at college, at the end of their freshman year, and at the end of their senior year.[8]

The differences were not only according to grade but also to race. As *Inside Higher Ed* reported, "Ranking the importance of promoting racial understanding on a four-point scale, African American students started off with the highest score (above 3.2), followed by Hispanics (just below 3.2), Asians (around 2.9) and whites (just under 2.5). All four groups were lower at the end of their freshman year, and lower as well by their senior year."[9] Researchers laid bare the naïve assumption that mixing students together would prompt an appreciation for racial diversity.

The findings of these researchers should have been expected because American universities were warned twenty years earlier about the need to anticipate the challenges that would arise from increasing campus diversity.[10] Their study of roughly four thousand students at

---

Allegations of Racial Bias and Illegal Campaign Activity," *The New Yorker*, December 21, 2017, www.newyorker.com/news/news-desk/a-conservative-nonprofit-that-seeks-to-transform-college-campuses-faces-allegations-of-racial-bias-and-illegal-campaign-activity.

[7] For a more developed argument on race and university ethics, see Keenan, "Diversity and Race," *University Ethics*, 149-172.

[8] Jesse Rude, Gregory C. Wolniak, Ernest T. Pascarella, "Racial Attitude Change during the College Years," Paper for the 2012 Annual Meeting of the American Educational Research Association (AERA) in Vancouver, British Columbia, www.norc.org/PDFs/AERA%20Annual%20Meeting/Racial%20Atttude%20Change%20during%20the%20College%20Years%20(AERA%202012).pdf.

[9] Scott Jaschik, "Backwards on Racial Understanding," *Inside Higher Ed*, April 10, 2012, www.insidehighered.com/news/2012/04/10/study-suggests-students-grow-less-interested-promoting-racial-understanding.

[10] Ernest T. Pascarella, Marcia Edison, Amaury Nora, Linda Serra Hagedorn and Patrick T. Terenzini, "Influences on Students' Openness to Diversity and Challenge in

eighteen institutions over the course of four years led them to make a variety of fundamental assertions about what a university needed to do to become a place that promotes racial understanding.

Mandating more culturally diverse classes alone was not the answer, though this was the route many colleges decided to choose. The problem with these courses was that students self-select along ethnic and racial lines in registering for them; thus, while they might *read* about diversity in such courses, they did not actually experience it. White students in one class never met the black students in the other. The researchers argued, instead, that occasioning conversations among students of diverse backgrounds on value-laden or controversial issues had a strong effect on all students. There students could realize that race is a construct and that many of their assumptions on significant political and cultural matters were informed by the same concerns. There and then they could learn that many of their impressions of other races were mistaken. Leaving them alone, however, only increased the negative stances from disinterest to suspicions and intolerance.[11]

Moreover, the researchers urged that beyond these student conversations, universities needed to commit themselves to promoting racial understanding as a good and that that good needed to be visible across the campus not only in particular classes but in the actual college culture. Universities need to invest themselves creatively in developing an across-the-university witness to the value of racial understanding.

What I found most interesting, however, were their concerns about the institutional policies. They discovered that the perception of a university's environment influenced their students' dispositions toward diversity. They recommended programs that sensitized faculty, administrators, and students to what constitutes racial discrimination and to couple that with clear evidence that such discrimination was never acceptable in campus life.[12]

Boasting diversity without having accompanying programs is a recipe for difficulties particularly for the newly arrived minorities. If the university wants a nondiscriminatory racial environment, it will not happen on its own; the administration will have to create the contexts for learning how diversity can work. As we have seen across America, racial mixing needs to have an agenda aimed at racial understanding. On campuses, the responsibility for this agenda falls to the

---

the First Year of College," *Journal of Higher Education* 67, no. 2 (1996): 174-195, 184.

[11] Pascarella, Edison, Nora, Hagedorn, and Terenzini, "Influences on Students' Openness to Diversity," 190-191.

[12] Pascarella, Edison, Nora, Hagedorn, and Terenzini, "Influences on Students' Openness to Diversity," 189.

administration. Administrators have largely underestimated these challenges, thinking that student-affairs or campus ministry could create these environments. If university presidents and their boards do not show that they are clearly opposed to racial discrimination, their inaction serves to validate those who actively or passively resist such attempts at integration. Administrators, with faculty, are going to have to invite students out of their self-selecting practices and into the habit of entering into more diverse environments.

Further studies show that, besides being the right thing to do, promoting diversity enhances student development. Where diversity functioned well, that is, at universities where students have diverse peers in the learning environment, their ability to engage in more complex thinking and to consider multiple perspectives improved. They concluded that "providing opportunities for quality interaction and an overall climate of support results not only in a better racial climate but also in important learning outcomes for students." In a word, diversity could actually be good news for educational goals.[13]

THE FIRST OBSTACLE TO CREATING A CULTURE OF UNIVERSITY ETHICS: THE ISOLATING INDIVIDUALISTIC WORLD OF THE FACULTY[14]

Twenty years ago, while editing a collection of essays on professional ethics for church ministry, I received from M. Shawn Copeland an essay not about the church but about the academy. Entitled "Collegiality as a Moral and Ethical Practice," she wrote about a young black woman theologian who found that her white colleagues were as strikingly naïve about their privilege as they were about her own challenges.[15] Copeland focused not only on their self-understanding but also on the isolating character of our training and our working in the academy. There and then, I began thinking first about university ethics and second about how highly individualistic the world of the faculty member is.

Unlike most professionals and civil servants, we university faculty function very much as individuals in the academy. Aside from department meetings, we study alone, work alone, teach alone, write alone, and lecture alone; we also grade students individually and write our

---

[13] Sylvia Hurtado, Jeffrey Milem, Alma Clayton-Pedersen, and Walter Allen, "Enacting Diverse Learning Environments: Improving the Climate for Racial/Ethnic Diversity in Higher Education," *ASHE-ERIC Higher Education Report* 26, no. 8 (1999): 6-7, files.eric.ed.gov/fulltext/ED430514.pdf.

[14] For more sustained treatment on these two obstacles see Keenan, "Cultural Landscape of the University Without Ethics," *University Ethics*, 57-79.

[15] M. Shawn Copeland, "Collegiality as a Moral and Ethical Practice," in *Practice What You Preach*, ed. James F. Keenan and Joseph Kotva (Lanham: Sheed and Ward, 1999), 315-332.

singular letters of recommendation. We cannot underestimate the individualism of our scholarly formation and our professional lifestyle. While almost every contemporary professional works in some form of partnership or team work—police officers with their partners, firefighters with their ladder companies, healthcare workers with their team, and lawyers with their firm—we faculty train alone and then work virtually alone.

Think of the dissertation. What other field of work requires its professional formation to be at least five years of working alone on one's own project with the last two years spent effectively in solitary confinement? Why is this, the highest expression of academic wisdom so individualistic and so isolationist?

Someone might say yes, but there is mentoring. However, even the relationality in the mentoring is not terribly thick. How many hours, during those four, five, or six years (35,040, 43,800, or 52,560 hours) do the advisor and mentee actually see and sit with one another? Is it at all analogous to other professional relationships where juniors literally shadow their mentor? Is this like other forms of mentorship?

One interesting corollary to the highly individualistic world we work in is found in the university's prescription that we write with a detached, inaccessible, frigid, dense style. An emotionally detached place like the academy trains us to be wary of writing anything accessible to others outside our field because it could compromise the style of a professorial reputation. Martin Anderson describes well academic publishing: "An academic book or a scholarly article is not expected to sell many copies, nor appeal to many people outside a select intellectual circle. Thus isolated, the typical academic intellectual operates freely, uninhibited by the judgment of outsiders, subject only to the verdict of colleagues who themselves are judged by the same narrow criteria."[16] But that style assures our elitism and privilege.

Certainly, many tenured faculty have great relationships with a variety of members of the university. My argument, however, is that, professionally speaking, there is not a structure that promotes those relationships. Teaching, grading, and mentoring are measured against singular professionals, but it is not just in those areas of university work that we are stand-alone individuals. Think, for instance, of office hours. What other professional corporate life lets their employees come to work whenever they want to? Other than the classes we teach and the occasional (monthly?) department meetings we may have to attend, we can choose to arrive for any office hours we want. Not only are we free to name our office hours, but there is rarely any expectation

---

[16] Martin Anderson, "The Isolation of the Academic Intellectuals Allows Their Natural Hubris to Flourish," *The Chronicle of Higher Education*, October 21, 1992, chronicle.com/article/The-isolation-of-the-academic/74347/.

to host office hours during any specific time that would be convenient to others. By office hours, we are required to be available to another person, presumably a student in need, yet we can set those hours whenever we want and rarely are we required to be there in the office for more than four or five hours a week. What other professional has such autonomy?

Note, I am not suggesting that faculty have only four hours of work. With teaching, letters of recommendations, publishing and other academic demands, many faculty have a full week of work, but that work is on our time, our place, and, again, usually alone. Hardly any other modern professional works this way. Still, we should be able to see that, when individual faculty take the initiative to enter into practices of solidarity with others, this can lead to the possibility of developing and sustaining an ethical community within the university. When faculty elect to join a seminar, volunteer to be on a university committee, offer to be the faculty advisor of student club, or host their class at home with a meal, they enter into relationships that make possible community. These turns to the practices of solidarity are themselves turns to ethical practices, and, with ethics, community can flourish. Without ethics, the community breaks down.

THE SECOND OBSTACLE: THE UNIVERSITY'S GEOGRAPHICAL LANDSCAPE

The isolating nature of the professoriate is well accommodated and protected from much of the lives of our students. As faculty, we do not know, as we once did, about our students' lives. We do not know where they live, whether they received merit or need based scholarships, nor do we know which ones have been hospitalized or arrested over the weekend. We only know about such issues incidentally. As Julie Reuben explains with the reforms of the late nineteenth century, faculty effectively withdrew institutionally from concerns about their students' private lives.[17] The faculty's ignorance of their students' personal lives is not only explained by the isolated nature of our present vocation, but also by the social contours of the university that do not foster community, friendship, or solidarity but rather departmentalizes personnel groupings routinely.

Just as faculty do not know much about their students, neither do other university employees know much about others at the so-called university. Plant managers, cafeteria workers, student affairs deans, financial aid officers, admissions boards, custodial workers, trustee members, campus ministers, university police, and librarians each have their own definable domain and their members know mostly

---

[17] Julie Reuben, *The Making of the Modern University: Intellectual Transformation and the Marginalization of Morality* (Chicago: University of Chicago Press, 1996).

what happens within that domain. Rarely are there occasions to go beyond one's domain (except when they go to university sporting events). The university might think of itself as a community, but it's a thin one at best.

Any reading of the literature on the life of the university tells us that the university's structure is very clear in its *vertical* direction; each cluster knows without a doubt who answers to whom in the upwardly-oriented structure of unilateral accountability. The university horizontally is not terribly clear, however, because its terrain is defined by departments unto themselves.[18] I think that the university's horizontal structure is best understood as fiefdoms, a perfect description of the university, inasmuch as both are deeply rooted in the medieval world. I believe that the university, stemming as it does from the medieval era, is affected structurally by its roots. Not only does its hierarchical structure make its accountability flow unilaterally and singularly vertically, but it also inherits the geography of fiefdoms that hinder matters not only of accountability and transparency but also of relationality, distributive justice, and the common good. There is very little horizontal accountability at the university.

Universities are organized by departments, a structure that gives the suggestion that each department shares something in common with another, but, given the hierarchical structures of the university, such a shared identity functions less in the operations and more in the purported mission design. Departments are part of the fiefdom structure, in part, because higher level administrators can treat departments differently without others in other departments knowing any differently. In fact, in many ways these administrators function as feudal lords. Life within the department is determined much less by what happens in other departments as by what happens between senior administrators and that department.

Fiefdoms are not only seen in academic departments but in student affairs as well. Just as faculty might not know the student's personal conduct, neither does student affairs know the student's academic life. Similarly, health and counseling services, development, alumni relations, athletics, dining services and many other departments function separately and are accountable to the different university managers, who make their own assessments according to their specific domain's criteria. In short, the standards, communications and information of each domain are not set across the university itself but are particular to and remain within the domain of the particular fiefdom. It is for this

---

[18] For a different line of thought, see Matthew Reisz, "The Seven Deadly Sins of the Academy" *Times Higher Education* September 17, 2009, www.timeshighereducation.co.uk/features/the-seven-deadly-sins-of-the-academy/408135.article.

reason that the only two constituencies who know what occurs across the university are the clients, that is the students, and the president.

In terms of ethics, this is fairly problematic because, as we know from Aristotle, there is some relationship between the *polis* or the actual community and the common good that makes possible human flourishment. To the extent that members of the polis as a society participate in and contribute to the common good, there is human flourishment. However, at the university, the players on the ground do not see a coherency in the community nor an operative notion of the common good.

The bureaucracy of the university does not have an internal horizontal structure of engagement nor are there any in-built structures of horizontal accountability within the university. Worse still, the bureaucracy of the university shows no sign of checking itself, continues expanding, and eventually will no longer be sustainable.[19] All these challenges prompt us to ask how we can overcome the obstacles to good community and provide a sharing of the common good. When we hear the hardships of adjunct faculty and when we see rising tuition (another unsustainable solution), coupled at the same time with expanding bureaucracies, their attendant appointments and competitive salaries, we realize that university's fiefdoms are very much the most compelling of all challenges.

Inasmuch as the university is partitioned by fiefdoms, so are the ethical issues. University critics tend to focus on one ethical issue, but they do not address other related ones. While student affairs are familiar with sexual assault and binge drinking, faculty are more familiar with cheating, and neither know really what athletics are doing with their athletes. These four topics remain in their own unconnected silos or fiefdoms. Similarly, only deans and department chairs usually know about the adjunct faculty, and few dare to address the responsibilities of the post-tenured faculty.

THE SCANDAL OF CONTINGENT FACULTY

Today, we distinguish between two types of faculty. On the one hand, there are the tenured faculty and those new professors who are hired to apply for tenure at the end of their 6-year track. On the other hand, there are those classified together as "contingent" or "adjunct faculty." They are contingent or adjunct to the tenured faculty, and, by all estimates, they now are the "New Faculty Majority" as an im-

---

[19] Benjamin Ginsberg, *The Fall of the Faculty: The Rise of the All-Administrative University and Why It Matters* (New York: Oxford University Press, 2013).

portant on-line resource and advocacy organization for contingent faculty calls itself.[20] Indeed, in America, there are more contingent faculty teaching than tenured and tenure-track faculty.

This situation is new. Since 1992, the average amount of time for tenured professors' teaching has diminished. As Derek Bok, former President of Harvard University notes, "The decline appears to have resulted from a reduction in the number of classroom hours required of the (tenured) faculty."[21] This reduction arose as a tradeoff for increased demands for tenured faculty to publish and to provide more and more administrative tasks.

Bok adds that emphasis on research has made faculty much more specialized, so "most faculty members prefer to teach the kinds of specialized courses and seminars that are aligned with their scholarly interests. Not surprisingly, teaching what professors know best does not always coincide with what undergraduates most need."[22] As a result, many of the fundamental courses that today's students need, like introductory and foundational ones, "core" courses, "Great Books" programs, and a host of other basic courses are taught by contingent faculty.[23]

In order to understand the matter of contingent faculty, we have to remember that adjuncts work as they do not because the work is lucrative but because they find teaching a rewarding profession. Still, some lament that they do not teach as well as tenured faculty, but that is inaccurate. In fact, a recent study from Northwestern University found "consistent evidence that students learn relatively more from non-tenure line professors in their introductory courses."[24]

We should also understand that the differences between full-time and part-time contingent faculty are remarkable. For years, universities have been hiring part-time contingent faculty and are only now in the process of doing it with any order and, in some places, rightly. For instance, a few major universities have recently provided greater professional and financial security to contingent faculty by hiring them full-time and providing them entry to a new system that parallels the tenured and tenure-track faculty. They have multi-year renewable contracts, promotions, merit increments, healthcare policies and, in some cases, voice and vote in the department.

---

[20] "Welcome to New Faculty Majority," *New Faculty Majority*, www.newfacultymajority.info/.
[21] Derek Bok, *Higher Education in America* (Princeton: Princeton University Press, 2013), 334.
[22] Bok, *Higher Education in America*, 334.
[23] Bok, *Higher Education in America*, 334.
[24] David Figlio, Morton Shapiro, and Kevin Soter, "Are Tenure Track Professors Better Teachers?" *National Bureau of Economic Research Working Paper No. 19406*, September 2013, www.nber.org/papers/w19406.

Most contingent faculty, however, are part-time. Many public and private universities and especially community colleges depend on contingent faculty who are willing to work according to whatever terms the college or university offers. Years ago, *The New York Times* provided the narrative of one typical part-time contingent faculty who taught nine courses in communications and public speaking at five different colleges. Her commute was about two hundred miles a week, and she either shared an office with sixteen other adjuncts or has no office at all.[25]

The stories of the impoverishment of contingent faculty are embarrassingly common. In 2012, *The Chronicle of Higher Education* said that these are stories of food stamps, welfare and Medicaid.[26] In 2013, CNN referred to contingent faculty as "the working poor."[27] The Democratic Staff Report of the House Committee on Education and the Workforce concluded their report in January 2014 writing, "In short, adjuncts and other contingent faculty likely make up the most highly educated and experienced workers on food stamps and other public assistance in the country."[28]

The development of adjunct faculty at any university is so related to supplementing the tenure-track faculty that university policies regarding adjunct faculty are, in many instances, *sui-generis*. Whatever contractual relationships, job responsibilities and security, and personnel benefits an adjunct has with one university will differ with the next university. Certainly, a similar insight can be said about tenure track faculty at a university; trying to understand their salaries, benefits, and responsibilities depends upon a variety of concerns at the given university. The university's decision is based on its perception of the "market" as well as its own interest or support of a particular area of a particular department. Thus, inasmuch as adjuncts are supplemental to the tenure-track faculty, all the more are a particular university's contracts with its adjuncts that particular university's construction. Such a reality reinforces my argument that universities give little attention

---

[25] Robbie Woliver, "Adjunct Professors: Low Pay and Hard Going," *New York Times* May 7, 2000, www.nytimes.com/2000/05/07/nyregion/adjunct-professors-low-pay-and-hard-going.html.
[26] Stacey Patton, "The Ph.D. Now Comes With Food Stamps," *The Chronicle of Higher Education*, May 6, 2012, chronicle.com/article/From-Graduate-School-to/131795/; Dean Dad, "Adjuncts on Food Stamps," *Inside Higher Ed*, May 8, 2012, www.insidehighered.com/blogs/confessions-community-college-dean/adjuncts-food-stamps.
[27] Gary Rhoades, "Adjunct Faculty are the New Working Poor," *CNN*, September 25, 2013, www.cnn.com/2013/09/24/opinion/rhoades-adjunct-faculty/index.html.
[28] U.S. House Committee on Education and the Workforce, Democratic Staff, *The Just-in-Time Professor* (Washington, DC: United States House of Representatives, January 2014), 34, democrats-edworkforce.house.gov/imo/media/doc/1.24.14-AdjunctEforumReport.pdf.

to ethical normative standards, a point quite apparent in the lack of any standards for the *majority* of university faculty.

Inasmuch as the university is so siloed or departmentalized, few know of any instances elsewhere at the university where the search for such standards might be happening. Since many tenured faculty live in a fairly non-horizontal accountability world, most do not know the actual working conditions that contingent faculty have. Their ignorance is further compromised (or protected) because university decision-making is marked by such a considerable lack of transparency and accountability. Not only that, every department has its own hiring policies that are decided by the dean; a department chair simply effectuates the dean's decisions, often not knowing how other departments proceed. Still, it is important to know that most tenured faculty do not (yet) show interest in the working conditions of their colleagues. Such is the situation today at colleges and universities that teach ethics but have not realized (yet) that *they* need to practice ethics.

INITIATING A CALL FOR SOLIDARITY

Let me begin by sharing a personal experience of coming clean about university ethics and contingent faculty. I want to invite you into the way I see things today by first acknowledging how I let myself stay unaffected. I want to come clean with you in closing, so as to suggest that you might do the same, for coming clean is, I think, the first step for working for a culture of ethics at a university.

In my sixteen years at Boston College, I have worked on faculty development, mentoring junior tenure-track faculty and developing programs for graduate students, from advising and mentoring to starting a culture of teaching formation in our doctoral program. When I was writing my book, I learned a lot about contingent faculty but next to nothing about the actual contingent faculty at my university or in my department. As I researched more and more, I realized that the gulf between tenured faculty and adjunct faculty has few secure ways of passage connecting us. Like other tenured faculty, I had un/consciously, but conveniently, worn blinders about their work and their context.[29] I managed to tell myself, they do not concern me. They do, but I managed to tell myself otherwise. At the same time, a journalist who is also a contingent faculty member, Lisa Liberty Becker, asked to interview me because she was writing on adjunct faculty and heard that I was writing this book on university ethics. In the course of the interview, she concurred that I had a pretty good handle on the issues that adjuncts face. Before we descended into the details, she asked me

---

[29] For a similar acknowledgement about the matter, see Peter D. G. Brown, "Confessions of a Tenured Professor," *Inside Higher Ed*, May 11, 2010, www.insidehighered.com/views/2010/05/11/confessions-tenured-professor.

an important question, "What do you know about adjunct faculty at your own institution?" "Next to nothing," I replied. "I have managed to tell myself, they do not concern me. Still, I'm acting chair next semester; assuredly I will find out."[30]

I make this confession simply to let the tenure-line faculty get some space to acknowledge that they probably, conveniently do not think about contingent faculty either. There is within the university structure a cultural myopia that allows us not to think about the contingent faculty. It is the fault of the structure of the university, but it is our fault too. Those same faults allow us to ignore issues of race, gender and class, student athletes, sexual assault, binge drinking, unsustainable tuition, unaccountable faculty and the rest.

If you resonated with my argument here, I ask you to consider how the university in its structure and how the professoriate in its vocation have given you the chance to pursue your own academic interests, without bothering you about a culture of ethics. If you can, think for a moment have you allowed yourself to settle into that complacency? And if you have, should you not admit that?

Recognizing how we really think of one another at the university strikes me as a worthy starting point for any discourse on university ethics. What is the second step? Get to know your contingent faculty. Here at Boston College, as I was finishing my book, I became the director of the Jesuit Institute, an Institute dedicated to fortifying issues of faith and culture on campus. With that mandate, I started several interdisciplinary faculty seminars there: Economic Inequity; Sustainability and *Our Common Home*; and Mental Health, Stigma, and Suffering. One seminar that I maintained from my predecessor was designed to introduce tenure track faculty to one another. In almost all these instances, the faculty participants were tenure line as they were in prior administrations.

I decided I wanted to innovate with a seminar for our full-time contingent faculty. Here, we use "Professors of the Practice" to identify our roughly 180 full-time contingent faculty. Here our administration has provided greater professional and financial security to contingent faculty by hiring them full-time and providing them entry to a new system that parallels the tenured and tenure-track faculty. They have multi-year renewable contracts, promotions, merit increments, healthcare policies, and, in some cases, voice and vote in the department. Mindful of our fiefdoms, I decided to invite eighteen well-known professors of the practice to a monthly seminar at the Jesuit Institute. The first meeting was like a homecoming. These faculty had been here on average at least twelve years, were now meeting each

---

[30] Lisa Liberty Becker, "Class Warfare," *Boston Magazine*, May 2014, www.bostonmagazine.com/news/article/2014/04/29/adjunct-professors-boston/.

other for the first time, and had the hope of meeting on a regular basis. They decided to name their seminar *The Jesuit Essentials* because their essential need at the university should be recognized.

They had not met one another because the occasions for many full-time contingent to meet fellow faculty outside the departments is rare. Still, one insight that emerged clearly. Though most Professors of the Practice do a fair amount of teaching, they also do a fair amount of administrative work, lecturing, and publishing. The diversity among the Professors of the Practice parallels that among the tenured faculty.

When my book *University Ethics* was published, *The Jesuit Essentials* made the book required reading for their seminar and then decided to host a conference on university ethics a year ago that brought 450 faculty and administrators to our campus coming from 45 different schools.[31] It was a great success connecting the ethical issues across the campus.

Since hosting the conference, our seminar is addressing a number of issues. One recent issue might give you an idea of how isolating the world of the department is and how it affects both professors of the practice and the tenure line faculty. We learned that, in one department, the executive committee together with the chair decided that in the recruitment of candidates for a newly-opened tenure-track-line in the department, only the tenured and tenure track faculty members had access to the candidates' applications. In fact, they decided that none of the contingent faculty would be informed of the job talks either. Effectively, the professors in this department did not know until word leaked out of a job talk that there were candidates. They returned to our seminar asking what the policies in the other departments were. They learned that some had policies and others did not and that some included contingent faculty in entry level recruitment even to the point of voting for the hire. They returned to their department with the data, and, eventually, the chair with both the professors of the practice and the tenure line faculty articulated a policy regarding hires that was more interested in equity than privilege.

Realizing that we share a common vocation, we tenure-line faculty might recognize that we need to overcome our isolating privileges so as to enter into greater solidarity with our growing cadre of "contingent" colleagues. As we do, our sense of privilege might be threatened, but I do not think that either our shared vocation or the university itself would be harmed at all by some intentional meetings among all the faculty that would focus on equity and solidarity. In fact, I suggest it

---

[31] "Toward a Culture of University Ethics: A Conference at Boston College April 5-7, 2017," *Boston College*, www.bc.edu/centers/jesinst/toward-a-culture-of-university-ethics.html.

might help us to overcome the obstacles that impede the university's flourishment in the first place.[32]

---

[32] Special thanks to Charles Power for his assistance in editing this essay.

Saying No to an Economy that Kills: Undermining Mission and Exploiting Vocation in Catholic Higher Education

Kerry Danner

MORAL THEOLOGIANS AND SOCIAL ETHICISTS are well trained in what constitutes human flourishing and communion with God and others. Yet, there is still surprisingly little work on how Catholic colleges and universities create obstacles to human flourishing in regard to their employment practices, particularly the rise in contingent faculty.[1] Currently, nearly 75 percent of college faculty members are contingent workers.[2] Still, many students and their parents do not realize this because most universities do not actively report this data to their own staff and faculty, much less to students and parents. To ignore this shift and the institutional policies that support it is nothing short of willful ignorance.[3] Those who attempt to deny the scope and harm of the current landscape of higher education are analogous to those who deny climate change. In almost all cases, contingent faculty labor funds the salaries of tenured and tenure track faculty, and yet contingent faculty often receive extraordinarily low comparative pay for similar work, no or limited access to benefits, and apathy or disdain from their colleagues. Without addressing the changed landscape of the U.S. economy and the professoriate and without rethinking the very structure of the academy, the small percentage of tenure-track faculty will, like those denying climate change, enjoy the privileges of their positions while simultaneously eroding the future of a profession they love. Catholic colleges and universities participating in such practices ig-

---

[1] I use the term contingent faculty to include those working part-time and those working full-time with renewable contracts. I use the term part-time faculty interchangeably with adjunct faculty to highlight those most likely to be receiving proportionately lower pay and no or low benefits when compared with full-time faculty of any category.
[2] The Coalition on the Academic Workforce, *A Portrait of Part-Time Faculty Members*, June 2012, www.academicworkforce.org/CAW_portrait_2012.pdf.
[3] The Coalition on the Academic Workforce, *A Portrait of Part-Time Faculty Members*.

nore Catholic social teaching and fall short of manifesting the distinctively Catholic charism to model evangelization that serves not only church members but also the world at large. Creating a culture of good news requires creating an economy of life, which supports the material and spiritual needs of workers. The hiring of contingent faculty in particular, and short-term workers without benefits more generally, undermines the mission of Catholic universities and colleges and exploits the vocation and the dignity of work.

I begin by placing the increase in contingent faculty in a larger economic context and then demonstrate how current business practices, including those at Catholic colleges and universities, are in tension with Catholic social teaching, undermining the good of persons, the stability of families and communities and obscuring employer responsibilities. The second section focuses specifically on contingent faculty and how current employment practices undermine an educational mission and exploit the vocation of the theologian, lay Catholic and the professoriate more generally. The third section focuses on tactics to move toward just pay, inclusion, and advocacy for contingent faculty and the need for Catholic universities and colleges not just to teach about Catholic social teaching but to model it in their culture and employment practices.

INCREASED TEMPORARY, LOW-WAGE WORK, DECREASED EMPLOYER RESPONSIBILITY

The U.S. economy has undergone profound shifts in the last forty years that have resulted in a shrinking middle class and unprecedented income disparity. This changed landscape speaks to an urgent need for the church to reclaim its deep and prophetic stance on the dignity of work and employer responsibility.[4]

Changed Economic and Institutional Landscape

In May 2017, Intuit's Brad Smith reported that roughly 34 percent of all U.S. jobs are gigs—short-term work without benefits—and that number is expected to rise to 43 percent by 2020.[5] While there are surely some who both have financial stability through other means and prefer the flexibility, most have to take these jobs because they are economically vulnerable. The gig economy is the culminating effect

---

[4] For a thorough explanation of Catholic higher education's labor challenges see Joseph McCartin's "Confronting the Labor Problem in Catholic Higher Education: Applying Catholic Social Teaching in an Age of Increasing Inequality" in the *Journal of Catholic Higher Education* 37, no. 1 (2018): 71-88.

[5] Patrick Gillepsie, "Intuit: Gig economy is 34 percent of US workforce," CNN-Money, May 24, 2017, money.cnn.com/2017/05/24/news/economy/gig-economy-intuit/index.html.

of changed business practices that deliberately try to evade long-term employer-employee relationships and responsibilities to persons from whose work they benefit.[6]

In the 1980s, business practices turned to identifying and streamlining core competencies, and increasing financial flexibility by relying on short-term and long-term contractors.[7] For the past forty years, growing numbers of corporate and nonprofit employers have distanced themselves from their workers in an effort to save costs and, in turn, obscure responsibility for their welfare. Not surprisingly, wage theft and income inequality have risen and savings have shrunk. The Department of Labor reported that weekly minimum wage violations in California and New York alone amounted to an estimated $1.6 to $2.5 billion of lost wages for workers in 2011.[8] While these numbers may be particularly high due to the levels of undocumented workers in these states, these estimates do not account for lost income due to unpaid overtime. Further, gig workers have to pay for their own healthcare, often resulting in lower quality and almost always more expensive care, have no paid vacation, resulting in increased psychological and physical stress, and earn lower wages and no access to employer matching, decreasing day to day and retirement savings. Roughly 57 percent of Americans had $1,000 or less in their savings account in 2017.[9] The Economic Policy Institute reported that in 2013 "high-income families [were] 10 times as likely to have retirement accounts as low-income families."[10]

Regarding income inequality, the average CEO-to-worker income ratio in 1980 was 42:1, but by 2014 that ratio had ballooned to 373:1.[11] Since the recession ended in 2009, more than half of all job growth

---

[6] See Nick Wertsch, "Just Employment on University Campuses" Presented at the United Association for Labor and Education 2016 Annual Conference, April 15, 2016, uale.org/document-table/conferences/conference-2016/425-just-employment-on-university-campuses/file. Wertsch and I developed our approach to these issues in parallel while working at Georgetown University.

[7] See David Weill, *The Fissured Workplace: Why Work Became So Bad for So Many and What Can Be Done to Improve It* (Cambridge: Harvard University Press, 2014).

[8] Ross Eisenbrey. "Wage Theft by Employers is Costing U.S. Workers Billions of Dollars a Year, *Economic Policy Institute*, www.epi.org/blog/wage-theft-by-employers-is-costing-u-s-workers-billions-of-dollars-a-year.

[9] Kathleen Elkins, "Here's How Much Money Americans Have in their Savings Accounts," *CNBC*, September 13, 2017, www.cnbc.com/2017/09/13/how-much-americans-at-have-in-their-savings-accounts.html.

[10] Monica Morrisey, "The State of American Retirement: How 401(k)s have failed most American workers," *Economic Policy Institute*, www.epi.org/publication/retirement-in-america.

[11] "Income Inequality," *Inequality.org*, inequality.org/facts/income-inequality/.

has been in low-wage work.[12] Workers have been subject to suppressed wages since the 1970s, earning only .2 percent more per hour now than then when adjusted for inflation.[13] There are, of course, many other factors for these changes. A decrease in unionization and worker protections, an increase in technological advances, the relaxation of regulations and lower corporate tax rates have all contributed to growing income inequality. Higher education is not exempt from any of these trends.

On-campus, many services such as bookstores, security, food service, and janitorial services have been increasingly outsourced.[14] Most of these jobs pay minimum or just over minimum wage. Even if jobs are not outsourced, on-campus jobs are often still low paying. In 2012, more than 700,000 university workers earned less than a living wage, and a significant percentage of food service, janitorial, groundskeeping and security workers did not earn enough to meet the federal poverty line of $24,300.[15] Meanwhile, between 1976-2011, senior university administrator positions grew by 141 percent.[16] "Full-time, non-professional employee ranks at colleges and universities grew 369 percent, while full-time, tenure and tenure-track ranks grew by just 23 percent."[17] Part-time positions increased by 286 percent and full-time non-tenure track faculty by 259 percent.[18] Over the same period, university CEOs' pay grew by 175 percent. The average course compensation for an adjunct is just $2,700 per course.[19] A congressional report, *The Just-in-Time Professor,* estimates there are over one million contingent faculty in the U.S.[20] Whether outsourced or low-paid staff,

---

[12] Mark Gongloff, "Half of All Jobs Created in the Past 3 Years Were Low Paying: Study," *Huffington Post*, May 13, 2013, www.huffingtonpost.com/2013/05/13/low-paying-jobs_n_3266737.html.
[13] Jay Shambaugh and Ryan Nunn, "Why Wages Aren't Growing in America," *Harvard Business Review*, October 24, 2017, hbr.org/2017/10/why-wages-arent-growing-in-america.
[14] David Milstone, "Outsourcing Services in Higher Education: Consider the Campus Climate," *The Bulletin* 79, no. 2 (2010): 30-39.
[15] Pablo Eisenberg, "Campus Workers' Wages: A Disgrace to Academe," *Chronicle of Higher Education*, September 10, 2012, chronicle.com/article/A-Living-Wage-for-Campus/134232.
[16] Colleen Flaherty, "Professor Pay Up 2.2%," *Inside Higher Ed*, April 7, 2014, www.insidehighered.com/news/2014/04/07/faculty-salaries-are-22-report-sees-many-financial-issues-facing-professors#sthash.lrdfznG4.dpbs.
[17] Flaherty, "Professor Pay Up 2.2%."
[18] Flaherty, "Professor Pay Up 2.2%."
[19] The Coalition of Academic Workforce, *A Portrait of Part-Time Faculty Members*.
[20] U.S. House Committee on Education and the Workforce, Democratic Staff, *The Just-in-Time Professor* (Washington, DC: United States House of Representatives, January 2014), democrats-edworkforce.house.gov/imo/media/doc/1.24.14-AdjunctEforumReport.pdf.

whether adjunct faculty member or janitor, university workers are often paid so little they are unable to adequately care for their material needs. Such restrictions impact their spiritual well-being, leaving them unable to partake in the life of the campus or wider community. On one hand, given the larger economic changes, the move to outsourcing and the related rise in income inequality in higher education is not that surprising. On the other hand, there are pointed reasons why Catholic universities and campuses in particular should resist these trends and reclaim ethically defensible economic models in higher education.

The documental history of Catholic social teaching clearly demonstrates the moral necessity of protecting the worker. Beginning with *Rerum Novarum,* and in numerous papal encyclicals and U.S. Bishops' statements since, the teaching of the church makes clear that persons must be put before profit. This message becomes more urgent in the current U.S. context as gig work continues to increase and workers have fewer opportunities to find full-time jobs with benefits.

Catholic Social Teaching on the Dignity of Work

Pope Francis writes in *Laudato Si',* "To stop investing in people, in order to gain greater short-term financial gain, is bad business for society" (no. 127). For support, he cites *Caritas in Veritate* (no. 32), where Pope Benedict reminds society of the need to "continue to prioritize the goal of access to steady employment for everyone" no matter the limited interests of business and dubious "economic logic." Francis reiterates the consistent link between the good of the human person and work. He writes, helping the "poor financially must always be a provisional solution in the face of pressing needs. The broader objective should always be to allow them a dignified life through work" (*Laudato Si',* no. 128). When employees or faculty have to forgo medical treatment due to its expense, have little or no day-to-day savings or retirement savings, and are unable to participate deeply in campus-life or the wider community, they do not have a life fully fitting the human person.

It has been almost forty years since *Laborem Exercens* was released, but its focus on the theology of work grounded in Scripture and the causes and remedies of worker exploitation remains as relevant now as it was then. John Paul II offered a sustained critique of the reification of the person in the labor market. According to him, work is a defining characteristic of humanity, and through it, humans participate in the creative activity of God to meet the needs of the community (no. 4, 24-27).[21] The value of work comes from the person

---

[21] See David Hollenbach, "Human Work and the Story of Creation: Theology and Ethics in *Laborem exercens,*" in *Co-creation and Capitalism: John Paul II's Laborem*

doing the work, the proper "subject of work" even when the "work" is mechanized (nos. 5-6) or, perhaps, even when the syllabus is already written or books selected. Worker solidarity is advocated, including an increase in worker participation, to protect humans in the face of the change, such as types, conditions and opportunities of work (nos. 7-8). Worker issues are fundamentally a Christian concern and must be addressed anew as circumstances change. The types, conditions and opportunities for work in higher education have changed, and Catholic universities and colleges have an obligation to protect the dignity of work and encourage and practice worker solidarity.

The human value that work generates is both participation in God's creative work and an opportunity to become closer to and more formed by God. Work is overall positive and fulfilling, and its dignity is related to imaging God; as Genesis shows us, humans too require work and rest (no. 25). Francis highlights the necessity of work as part of a full life: "Work should be the setting for this rich personal growth, where many aspects of life enter into play: creativity, planning for the future, developing our talents, living out our values, relating to others, giving glory to God" (*Laudato Si'*, no. 127). Low-paid workers, workers marginalized from community life through contract work, and workers juggling multiple jobs to make ends meet are distanced from life-enriching rest and community (USCCB, *Economic Justice for All*, no. 14). Planning for the future is harder when one is worried about paying today's bills. Developing one's talents is stunted when one's position has no growth potential. In short, employers must meet the material needs of their workers so that their spiritual needs have a greater chance of being met too.

In *Laborem Exercens,* John Paul II traces the development of worker solidarity since the promulgation of *Rerum Novarum* to demonstrate how the emerging liberal-political system favored capital over labor. *Laborem Exercens* insists on the priority of labor over capital, critiquing this system that seeks maximum profit while attempting to pay the lowest possible wage and disregard the safety, health and living conditions of workers and their families (nos. 11-12). To right this imbalance, worker solidarity emerged as a response to the degradation and exploitation first experienced by industrial workers (no. 8). Workers should have an opportunity to share in the means of production, management, or benefits from profit sharing (nos. 14-15). Labor rights include "suitable employment for all who are capable of it" (no. 18), just remuneration for the work done, including a family wage, and a labor process conducive to human needs (nos. 18-19), the right to

---

exercens, ed. John Houck and Oliver Williams, CSC (Washington D.C: University Press of America, 1983), 59-77.

form unions (no. 20), and the right to emigrate in search of work (no. 23).

Paying a family wage and supporting workers' rights have been consistently taught in Catholic social thought and show up in papal encyclicals and U.S. Bishops' statements.[22] Such teaching makes clear that, when employers depress wages, they limit worker agency and harm the common good. "If through necessity or fear of a worse evil the workman accepts harder conditions because an employer or contractor will afford no better, he is made the victim of force and injustice" (*Centesimus Annus*, no. 8). Later social teaching addresses needs for retirement, health insurance, and even accident or disability insurance (*Quadragesimo Anno,* no. 14; *Centesimus Annus*, no. 24. Thus, Catholic social thought is clear that reliance on short-term and contract workers to avoid paying living wages and providing social protections for workers is ethically indefensible.

Laborem Exercens contributes to a deeper understanding of the reality of workers by discussing the responsibilities of the direct and indirect employer and role of intermediary organizations. Direct employers are always accountable for respecting the rights of the worker (no. 17). The state is considered an "indirect" employer by substantially determining "one or other facet of the labor relationship" and helping the direct employer establish an ethically correct labor policy (no. 17). Universities and colleges function as direct employers. Gerald Beyer demonstrated how Catholic universities and colleges' attempts to block adjunct unions selectively ignores the contexts in which unions become necessary and contributes to the undermining of universities and colleges' mission through neglect of Catholic social teaching.[23] Regarding Beyer's first point, unions are a long-standing mechanism for raising wages generally and for contingent faculty specifically. Unionized adjuncts earned roughly 25 percent more in pay across most university types, with the exception of baccalaureate colleges, according to a 2012 survey by the Coalition on the Academic Workforce.[24] The same survey indicates that unionized faculty are significantly more likely to have access to healthcare and retirement benefits, including retirement matching. Unions are acting as a corrective force to unjust employers who are depressing contingent faculty wages. Beyer's second point—that Catholic universities and

---

[22] See *Laborem Exercens*, no. 19; *Quadragesimo Anno,* no. 14; *Centesimus Annus*, no. 24; USCCB's *Statement on Church and Social Order* and *Economic Justice for All.*

[23] Gerald J. Beyer, "Labor Unions, Adjuncts, and the Mission and Identity of Catholic Universities" *Horizons* 42, no. 1 (2015): 1-37.

[24] The national median adjunct pay for a three-credit course is $2,700, $2,475 for nonunionized part-time faculty and $3,100 for unionized part-time faculty. See The Coalition of Academic Workforce, *A Portrait of Part-Time Faculty Members*.

colleges are undermining mission—is clear by these institutions' selective engagement, application, and promotion of Catholic social thought.

Rerum Novarum acknowledges that the state itself cannot solve every aspect of various social problems and thus, intermediary organizations, such as family and various cultural and economic and political groups, help to realize human fulfillment. Religion, more narrowly the Catholic Church, is highlighted for its important role in promoting justice. There is "no intermediary more powerful than religion (whereof the Church is the interpreter and guardian) in drawing the rich and the working class together, by reminding each of its duties to the other, and especially of the obligations of justice" (no. 19). Catholic universities and colleges are employers whose mission stems from the church; they function as both direct employers and as intermediary organizations. They have a particular responsibility to fulfill both obligations by modeling just pay and social protections for their own workers. Instead, they are undermining their mission and exploiting vocations, particularly regarding contingent faculty.

UNDERMINING MISSION, EXPLOITING VOCATION

As James Keenan points out in his 2015 *University Ethics*, the ethical and moral power of universities—real or aspirational—is currently questionable at best. By and large universities have failed to create "a culture of ethical consciousness and accountability."[25] Keenan points to the "silo" effect of departments, which leads to all kinds of horizontal bubbles, where faculty may know few other faculty or employees. In the *Journal of College and Character*, Laura Harrison notes that, when people do leave their silos, they tend to do so "in a competitive context" often pitted against each other in a "discourse that separates us."[26] Classism against blue-collar workers and racism often create additional barriers to getting to know one another.[27] A matrix of pressures—widespread economic trends, the nature of academic work, the organization of higher education, and classism and racism—have become obstacles to fulfilling universities and colleges' missions.

Undermining Mission

Addressing the current matrix of pressures is necessary for higher education to reclaim its moral power and to impact positively the lives

---

[25] James Keenan, S.J. *University Ethics: How Colleges Can Build and Benefit from a Culture of Ethics* (Lanham: Rowman & Littlefield, 2015), 4.
[26] Laura M. Harrison, "Faculty and Student Affairs Collaboration in the Corporate University," *Journal of College and Character* 14, no. 4 (2013): 365-372, 367.
[27] Eisenberg, "Campus Workers' Wages: A Disgrace to Academe."

of the campus community and fulfill institutional mission. Most higher education institutions are anchors for their communities, "whose physical presence is integral to the social, cultural, and economic wellbeing of the community."[28] The 4,000-plus colleges and universities in the United States "*spend* more than $400 billion annually, *own* more than $300 billion in endowment investments, and *employ* roughly three million faculty and staff."[29] The economic and social reach of higher education is formidable. Further, community engagement is often an explicit component of university mission statements, strategic plans and curriculums, so important that community partnerships are frequently tracked and evaluated.[30]

We are faced with a climate wherein current business practices are undermining institutions' educational mission but also their contributions to the common good and as anchor institutions in their local communities. By and large, anchor institutions, such as hospitals and universities, offer extensive tangible and intangible benefits to employees, including quality health care, retirement matching, and tuition. But as Laura Harrison points out, "When these anchor institutions outsource jobs or increase part-time employees to circumvent such investments in human capital they harm the very communities they otherwise profess to support."[31]

All universities, by nature of their nonprofit status and mission, aim to strengthen knowledge, values, and positively impact the world. Catholic institutions, in addition to their nonprofit and anchor status, often have mission statements that expressly commit themselves to social justice and the common good. To the extent such institutions have outsourced staff or created tenuous employment of faculty, they have lost moral credibility. This is particularly true for Catholic institutions that ignore Catholic social teaching on labor and the dignity of work.

Low and unstable work offered to so many contingent faculty members undermines the value of education and the production of knowledge. First, the underpaying of faculty devalues the very worth of a college degree. Contingent faculty members receive the very smallest fraction of tuition dollars of all faculty members. One has to

---

[28] Debra Friedman, David Perry, and Carrie Menendez, "The Foundational Role of Universities as Anchor Institutions in Urban Development: A Report of National and Data Survey Findings," *Association of Public and Land Grant Universities*, usucoalition.org/images/APLU_USU_Foundational_FNLlo.pdf.

[29] Rita Axelroth Hodges and Steve Dubb, *The Road Half Traveled: University Engagement at a Crossroads* (East Lansing: Michigan State University Press, 2012), 7. Emphasis mine.

[30] Friedman, Perry, and Menendez, "The Foundational Role of Universities as Anchor Institutions in Urban Development."

[31] Harrison, "Faculty and Student Affairs Collaboration," 367.

question, if the education provided is not worth professional compensation, is the degree itself?

Moreover, the growing move to a distinction between teaching and research faculty is deeply problematic. If, on average, only 25 percent of faculty are paid to do research, how will this affect the production of knowledge? Without financial support, few contingent faculty have the time and resources to commit to research and publication. Will only those with independent resources be able to publish in the humanities? Catholic universities and colleges are to ensure that "*university teachers* should seek to improve their competence and endeavour to set the content, objectives, methods, and results of research in an individual discipline within the framework of a coherent world vision" (*Ex Corde Ecclesiae*, no. 21). If faculty do not receive support to conduct research or even to keep up on current research, how can they fulfill this aspect of mission?

There are about 260 Catholic colleges and universities in the U.S., serving roughly 891,000 students.[32] While slightly over half of these students self-identify as Catholic, 79 percent have attended Catholic primary or secondary school.[33] Seventy-seven percent of students leave Catholic institutions believing "helping the poor or disadvantaged should be a life goal."[34] The reality is that many contingent faculty members at Catholic universities are the poor today, and students and parents have little awareness of how these institutions undermine their mission through hypocrisy.

Ex Corde Ecclesiae, no. 13, identified four essential characteristics of Catholic colleges. These essential characteristics are:

1. a Christian inspiration not only of individuals but of the university community as such;
2. a continuing reflection in the light of the Catholic faith upon the growing treasury of human knowledge, to which it seeks to contribute by its own research;
3. fidelity to the Christian message as it comes to us through the Church;
4. an institutional commitment to the service of the people of God and of the human family in their pilgrimage to the transcendent goal which gives meaning to life.

---

[32] Catholic Higher Education FAQs, *Association of Catholic Colleges and Universities*, www.accunet.org/Catholic-Higher-Ed-FAQs.

[33] Catholic Higher Education FAQs, *Association of Catholic Colleges and Universities*.

[34] Catholic Higher Education Embracing Social Justice, *Association of Catholic Colleges and Universities*, www.accunet.org/Portals/70/Images/Publications-Graphics-Other-Images/CHE-socialjustice.jpg?ver=2017-05-08-142606-590.

When these characteristics are considered in light of the material and spiritual situation of contingent faculty, Catholic universities and colleges' fidelity to the Christian message is lacking. Without the ability to participate fully in the life of the community and pursuit of truth and knowledge through stable paid study and research, people and mission suffer.

The Material and Spiritual Needs of Contingent Faculty

Contingent faculty members encounter multiple personal and institutional obstacles to meeting their material and spiritual needs. Before considering these factors however, three persistent myths must be addressed. The first is that contingent faculty members fill temporary departmental needs. This is simply not true the great majority of the time. The 2012 study by the Coalition on Academic Workforce found "over 80 percent of part-time faculty respondents reported having taught as a contingent faculty member for at least three years; over 55 percent taught in that role for six or more years, and over 30 percent for ten or more years."[35] This is critical to understanding the changed landscape of higher education: 80 percent of adjuncts have been at their institutions three years or longer.[36] The second myth is that most adjuncts have other jobs and do not rely on teaching as their sole income. While this is certainly sometimes the case, and there will be variation among universities and colleges, 73.3 percent of adjuncts polled in 2012 indicated that they considered teaching in higher education their primary employment.[37] The third and most persistent myth is firmly entrenched in the minds of many well-meaning people due to the connotation of the word adjunct itself. This is the myth that adjuncts are not core staff and are supplemental to the university. The idea of part-time faculty as adjunct—as supplementary and not essential—is fundamentally false. At Georgetown University there are nearly 1,100 part-time faculty, 224 non-tenure line full-time and 544-tenure line faculty.[38] Part-time faculty are essential faculty but have

---

[35] American Federation of Teachers, "A National Survey of Part-Time/Adjunct Faculty," *American Academic* 2 (2010), 8. See also The Coalition of Academic Workforce, *A Portrait of Part-Time Faculty Members*.

[36] I have worked part-time teaching a two/two course load for the past seven years as of fall 2018. Tenured-track faculty at Georgetown teach either a two/one or a two/two; Non-tenure full-time faculty teach a three/three course load.

[37] The Coalition of Academic Workforce, *A Portrait of Part-Time Faculty Members*.

[38] A few readers may want to point out that some of the 1,100 adjunct faculty at Georgetown University have other jobs. That misses the point. Nearly 70 percent of faculty members are contingent (working full-time on one, three or five year contracts and part-time on a semester by semester basis); 59 percent are adjunct (part-time). If roughly two-thirds of faculty have no benefits, cannot compete for internal funding and have no office space, clearly mission is affected. Universities and colleges have

been marginalized due to hiring practices, low pay, and lack of institutional support.

Part-time faculty pay is notoriously low, and some part-time faculty members work at multiple institutions to meet their financial needs. Rarely are there mechanisms for merit rewards or automatic Cost of Living Adjustments (COLA). Even when a department chair wants to raise pay, the dean or provost's office can thwart his or her efforts. Most institutions calculate a low hourly estimate per three-credit course to come up with a full-time equivalency percentage that avoids paying benefits. In most cases, faculty work far beyond this amount. To avoid paying benefits, institutions hire more adjuncts, often defending this decision on the basis of giving more people teaching experience. However, such experience is irrelevant when there are simply not enough full-time or tenure-track jobs. Some adjuncts have to reapply for their job every year; few have multiple year contracts, leaving them in near constant anxiety about being rehired. Low wages, income instability, and lack of the most basic employee benefits are also sources of stress on part-time faculty. Only 28 percent of adjuncts receive healthcare from their institutions.[39] More often than not institutions expect part-time faculty to pay for health care themselves or to have access to benefits from a partner. This latter practice relies on an employee being partnered and being partnered to someone with a job with benefits. In the former, part-time faculty members pay disproportionate amounts of their own income to obtain health care on the market.[40] Part-time faculty rarely have sick pay or maternity leave. They rarely have retirement matching, and, if they do, it is done on the basis of one's income and will be disproportionately low. Most cannot access tuition remission. Most cannot compete for internal grants and funding and will lose their part-time positions if external funding is obtained. In short, adjuncts work with no economic safety net, and institutions make no investment in adjunct well-being or professional growth.

Hiring practices for adjuncts set up a framework for marginalization. Adjuncts may or may not be interviewed, and, more often than not, no one other than the department chair is involved. (This is often

---

focused on positive effects of employing faculty with experience outside of the academy while ignoring the harm to faculty themselves, students and community.

[39] Of these 28 percent of adjuncts that reported receiving healthcare, 42 percent worked at public four-year institutions and just a third worked at private four-year institutions, see The Coalition of Academic Workforce, *A Portrait of Part-Time Faculty Members*.

[40] Since my partner's field also has moved to a contract model and few companies offer benefits, we purchase our healthcare on the market for $1500 per month. Three-quarters of my pay goes to cover my family's healthcare. Our monthly premium has risen roughly $250 per month in 2016, 2017 and 2018.

also the case for full-time faculty working on annual contracts.) Adjuncts are rarely introduced to the rest of departmental staff, much less the dean. By and large, tenure-track faculty do not feel invested in part-time workers—they do not know their credentials and, sometimes, do not care. Often, even after years of employment, part-time faculty members are not seen as colleagues but as temporary employees. Most adjuncts do not have offices. Many do not appear in directories, have business cards, or even access to letterhead. They may or may not be invited to staff meetings and are almost never invited to staff retreats. Sometimes departments rely only on course evaluations to assess adjunct performance, with few, if any, classroom observation or considerations of other types of contributions. Other adjuncts may be over-managed, enduring near constant assessment. For example, adjunct faculty employed by the 14 regional state colleges making up the Pennsylvania State System of Higher Education are reviewed five times per academic year.[41] When and if full-time faculty positions open up, it is rare for an adjunct to be hired. The lack of material and spiritual support undermines the good of workers, and, in turn, undermines the good of their families and ability to contribute to the larger community. The Christian message of good news is replaced by economic anxiety and isolation; the pursuit of truth and knowledge is stunted.

Exploitation by the Market

During a 2018 panel at the Annual Meeting of Society of Christian Ethics, Jason King argued that the move toward the hiring of contingent faculty is motivated by Catholic universities' and colleges' quest for survival.[42] He pointed to the business practices (and pressures) of 1) remaining financially viable; 2) attracting students and parents; 3) controlling costs through increased donations and cutting salaries, and 4), and perhaps most troubling, the valuing of administrators over faculty. As already noted, these last two points appear across the university landscape. However, in truth, many universities, even Catholic ones, have a long history of paying poverty or near poverty wages. What has changed is who is receiving them. These changed business practices and their impact on teaching as a profession and the real or perceived fiscal pressure continue to undermine mission.

---

[41] See the Agreement Between Association of Pennsylvania State College and University Faculties (APSCUF) and The Pennsylvania State System of Higher Education (State System) July 1, 2015, to June 30, 2018, 26, www.apscuf.org/contracts/APSCUFfacultyCBA2015-18.pdf.

[42] Jason King, "Contingent Faculty and the Heart of Catholic Education," Presented at the Society of Christian Ethics, Portland, Oregon, January 6, 2018.

These business practices include exploiting a labor pool that these schools have helped to create. There are 26 doctoral degree-granting programs in theology and religious studies that create the market. From 2006-2016, there have been about 6,050 doctoral degrees conferred in biblical studies, Judaic studies, religious studies, and theology/theological education.[43] Every year since 2010, there were between 560 and 613 degrees conferred. In that same period, anywhere from 184 to 232 job advertisements per year were placed at the American Academy of Religion/Society of Biblical Literature Employment Center for assistant-level full-time positions, which included one-year and non-tenure-track appointments. In 2016, fewer than 300 jobs were posted, at any level, the lowest since 2002.[44] While postgraduate statistics are only available from the National Science Foundation (NSF) every five years, their data confirms a similar trend. The 2006, 2011, and 2016 statistics show a downward shift from 66.7 percent to 52.1 percent in the rate of a recent PhD having a "definite placement." However, NSF's placement numbers also include post-doctorates, full-time non-tenure line positions, jobs outside of the academy, and potentially adjunct work, making these placement rates significantly lower.

According to the American Academy of Religion's employment trend report there has been anywhere from a high of thirty three (2016) to a low of thirteen (2012) advertisements for Christian ethics positions, of any rank and type, in the past ten years. Catholic universities and colleges advertise the majority of these positions, as they tend to require courses in theology and religious studies. While the numbers need more rigorous tracking and analysis, it is clear that there are simply too many qualified candidates for too few jobs and that the market becomes increasingly flooded every year. Moreover, if one has care-giving responsibilities or otherwise cannot move for a one-year appointment, the chances of acquiring full-time academic work decline. Every chair and graduate advisor, and certainly every incoming graduate student, should understand the complexities of the current environment. Administrators continually defend low per course compensation based on market conditions, even though Catholic social teaching clearly rejects such appeals. In *Mater et Magistra,* John XXIII wrote:

---

[43] Data compiled from "Table 13: Degrees Granted by Subfield 2004-2014," *National Science Foundation*, www.nsf.gov/statistics/2016/nsf16300/data-tables.cfm.
[44] Job Advertisement Data 2015-2016, American Academy of Religion and Society of Biblical Literature, www.aarweb.org/sites/default/files/pdfs/Career_Services/AARSBLJobsReport2015-2016.pdf.

> We therefore consider it our duty to reaffirm that the remuneration of work is not something that can be left to the laws of the marketplace; nor should it be a decision left to the will of the more powerful. It must be determined in accordance with justice and equity; which means that workers must be paid a wage which allows them to live a truly human life and to fulfill their family obligations in a worthy manner. (no. 71)

The current situation, in its clear exploitation of market conditions, is made worse through an exploitation of vocation.

Exploitation of Vocation

An often-overlooked factor in conversations about contingent faculty, whether from the perspectives of contingent faculty themselves, tenured or tenure-track allies or administrators, is the powerful narratives, some more true than others, about vocation. Most people pursue doctoral degrees in theology because they not only want to do so, they feel called to do so by their skills and interest and relationship with God. Both the spiritual and professional aspects of vocation highlight what makes the current landscape of higher education so ripe for exploitation.

The term vocation shows up nearly fifty times in the *Catechism of the Catholic Church*, and its recurrent theme is the interdependence of personal and humanity's vocation to union with God. Most of those who choose to commit to doctoral studies in theology have discerned that study, teaching and research are the way to foster communion with God for themselves and others. Catholic contingent faculty (even more so those with doctoral degrees in theology) are likely to know and be committed to the teaching of *Lumen Gentium*,

> Upon all the laity, therefore, rests the noble duty of working to extend the divine plan of salvation to all [people] of each epoch and in every land. Consequently, may every opportunity be given them so that, according to their abilities and the needs of the times, they may zealously participate in the saving work of the Church. (no. 33)

Catholics may exhibit an even greater willingness to labor under unjust conditions *for* the church. Those faculty members familiar with the founding and maintaining of Catholic higher education will know the sacrifices made for its existence. Vowed religious men and women shouldered much of this sacrifice to found the great majority of our Catholic universities and colleges. Such commitment should and does inspire gratitude, but, when the bulk of faculty members are or will be married with families, the burden of fidelity to Catholic identity and evangelization is heavy indeed. It blurs what faculty expects of themselves and what we expect of our colleagues. For many of us, teaching theology or teaching at a Catholic university or college is an act of fidelity, an act of fidelity I fear many administrators are unconsciously willing to exploit.

Many colleges and universities neither compensate nor support the majority of their own faculty as professionals anymore. One may have a vocation to teach in a secular sense, but most university and college faculty members are no longer part of the professional class. Mary Crane writes,

> The reality is that for many, being a professor in America can no longer be considered a middle class job, which involves a significant shift in how we understand the vocation: A professor belongs to the professional class, a professor earns a salary and owns a home, probably with a leafy yard, and has good health insurance and a retirement account. In the American imagination, a professor is perhaps disheveled, but as a product of brainy eccentricity, not of penury. In the American university, this is not the case.[45]

Crane's point is that the link in the imagination between the vocation of being a professor and its ability to yield the economic benefits thought of as a professional's has persisted while the reality is broken. Nonetheless, the burdens of being a professional remain, particularly with regard to the structure of compensation and expectations of self and others. Part-time faculty are not paid an hourly wage but neither are they paid a professional wage. They meet with students until their questions are answered, grade papers until they are done, and review potential course material. While Mary McCartney is writing about medical school, her description is alarmingly accurate about the reality of the majority of today's faculty: "In the end, vocation is what it's all about. We're tested on its presence before we enter [a doctoral program]. We're implored to hold ourselves to the highest standards. *We're judged according to these standards, even when the resources to achieve them are willfully withheld.*"[46] In short, part-time faculty are held to professional standards but not supported by their institutions in this capacity. Yet, a strong sense of professional—and often religious or secular vocation—remains. Perhaps this is even more so if we love to teach and research, are invested in the project of higher education, or have simply invested so many years, and perhaps debt, in pursuit of our vocation to God, the church and the academy.

---

[45] Mary Crane, "Stop Defending the Liberal Arts," *Inside Higher Ed*, January 17, 2011, as cited by Marc Cortez, "Theological Vocation and the Academy" *Journal of Markets & Morality* 18, no. 2 (2015): 429–437, 429.
[46] Mary McCartney, "Vocation, Vocation, Vocation," *BMJ: British Medical Journal* (2016): 355, dx.doi.org/10.1136/bmj.i6526. Emphasis mine.

The hope of affirmation from these institutions is persistent. There are stories that work to foster hope for just employment: someone we know began as an adjunct and ultimately got a tenure-track position or an adjunct got hired full-time. Such stories are the *exception*, and they favor those without partners, without primary care-giving responsibilities, and with independent sources of wealth. The reality is that more often than not contingent faculty members are viewed as not being good enough or not wanting a tenure-track job enough. In regards to the study of ethics and the mission of Catholic higher education, this is painfully ironic for contingent faculty: lived fidelity to people and communities harms your career.

I have heard, more often than I would like to, department heads or administrators explain that adjunct teaching is a career stepping stone.[47] The argument goes that it provides much-needed teaching experience for adjuncts to obtain full-time positions. This is simply fallacious. As noted above, every year in which one is not hired, one becomes less competitive. Further, some institutions limit the number of years an adjunct can work for a university or college. To whose benefit is such a policy? Clearly it is not a benefit for the worker, students, or wider community, particularly when another adjunct will simply take that worker's place. Frederick Buechner famously said that vocation is the "place where your deep gladness and the world's deep hunger meet."[48] Students are hungry for passionate, committed faculty and, often, ignorant about adjunct work conditions. Institutions are hungry too, perhaps even gluttonous, and often do not show care in what (or who) gets consumed to meet their hunger. Without a commitment to systemic change, contingent faculty members will continue to be food for hungry universities, quickly devoured and expelled when too old or enrollment dips. The challenge then is to relieve the burdens of contingent faculty without simultaneously normalizing contingent faculty to the point of easy acceptance of unjust and damaging practices that undermine mission and exploit vocation.

Tactics to Reclaim Integrity and Promote Solidarity

I have argued that temporary, low-paid work with few benefits is ethically indefensible from the standpoint of both Catholic social teaching and the specific role and mission of Catholic universities and

---

[47] I have had many opportunities to discuss these issues directly with department heads and indirectly through panel discussions. For the past four years, I have worked with American Academy of Religion's Academic Labor and Contingent Faculty Working Group on these issues and served on their Board of Directors to represent contingent faculty concerns.

[48] Jordan J. Pallor, "Editorial," *Journal of Markets & Morality*, 18, no. 2 (2015): 251–254, 254. Pallor is referring to Frederick Buechner, *Wishful Thinking: A Seeker's ABC* (New York: Harper & Row, 1973), 95.

colleges. For the good of workers and the church, efforts must be taken to provide just pay, promote inclusion and increase advocacy of contingent faculty. Faith and solidarity require it.

Providing Just Pay, Accessing Benefits, Creating Job Security

How does one figure out what just pay is? Since these issues are so complex, I focus only on a few obstacles here. It is common knowledge that as tenure-line or tenured faculty in research universities, faculty members are to spend one-third of their time teaching, one-third on research and one-third on service. However, to my knowledge, we do not know how much this is actually practiced. Often, research is done during breaks and summer; this is particularly true when teaching loads are high. Actual time spent on research and service ebbs and flows from week to week and year to year. Further, sometimes research rates decline after tenure. My point is that this formula itself may need to be rethought. Second, it is common for faculty teaching in the humanities to be paid significantly less than those paid in the sciences due to an appeal to the market, even though doing so to avoid paying a just wage is contrary to Catholic social teaching. Fundamentally, any attempts by higher education administrators to justify low adjunct pay undermines the very value of the education the same institution is offering its students. Such rationalizations need to be constantly challenged.

Contingent faculty advocates suggest a just compensation would be between $10,300-$15,000 per three-credit course depending on the local cost of living and comparative full-time faculty pay.[49] These levels of pay include compensation for benefits, including health and retirement, which an institution is not paying through other means. While many struggling institutions balk at such suggestions, it is simply false to say money is not available if other faculty receive disproportionately more pay and/or staff and coaches receive such. Administrators must realign spending with mission, potentially readjusting other pay scales and spending.

I am not convinced that advocating for additional tenure lines or full-time contract lines is a tactic that promotes security or welfare for contingent faculty. More often than not, if a department is granted an

---

[49] The Modern Language Association's recommendation on minimum per-course compensation for part-time faculty members was $10,300 for 2017-2018. See "MLA Recommendation on Minimum Per-Course Compensation for Part-Time Faculty Members," *Modern Language Association*, www.mla.org/Resources/Research/Surveys-Reports-and-Other-Documents/Staffing-Salaries-and-Other-Professional-Issues/MLA-Recommendation-on-Minimum-Per-Course-Compensation-for-Part-Time-Faculty-Members. The Service Employees International Union, which represents 54,000 faculty in higher education, launched their $15K per course campaign in April 2015.

additional tenure or non-tenure line, a national search is conducted and preference is given to younger scholars with more publications and fewer years on the market. The adjuncts' fidelity and service to the institution with little pay, most often little investment in their growth as a teacher and no material support for publications, harms them in the job search. This is a painful and unjust reality of the current job market. Contingent faculty members are deemed good enough to teach a department's students, often for years, but, when a professional salary, benefits, and material resources needed to flourish or research are at stake, they are not "good enough." Not only is it demoralizing, it is very difficult to parse out how ageism, departmental or larger politics, or even personality factors into such decisions. The institution offers no fidelity to the worker. For these reasons, the more just tactic is to offer permanent part-time work with benefits and to create pathways for movement from adjunct to full-time and even adjunct or full-time non-tenure to tenured positions. Doing so acknowledges part-time faculty members existing contributions and professionalism.

In addition to raising pay, there are other ways that the welfare of part-time faculty can be addressed. Make sure they can access subsidized health care benefits and/or lower the threshold for when access can be reached. Universities and departments could set up preferred hiring status for other work at the university, changes that would allow many part-time instructors to gain desperately needed benefits, raise their compensation, and access retirement matching and tuition remission. In doing so, however, extra care has to be given to how to protect the academic freedom of the faculty member while also a staff member.[50] Create permanent part-time positions which offer just pay, access to COLA increases and merit rewards, and proportional benefits. Annual contracts should certainly be offered. Yet multiple year appointments provide better stability for the faculty member themselves, and the students, department, and wider campus community.

There are often differing visions of how best to respond to the rise in contingent faculty within departments. A common practice is to reinforce hierarchy based on labor category. Alternatively, universities could treat all faculty members equally. Or, finally, there is a preferential option for the most economically vulnerable.[51] I demonstrate

---

[50] See Lincoln Rice's essay on academic freedom and contingency in this volume.
[51] Jason King, "Contingent Faculty and the Heart of Catholic Education," and Elizabeth Hinson-Hasty, "Faculty Advocate and Middle Manager: Leveraging Privilege for the Sake of the University Common Good," presented at the Society of Christian Ethics, Portland, Oregon, January 6, 2018.

how this might work out in two areas: scheduling courses and distributing summer school courses.[52] Are the preferences of tenure line and tenured faculty given priority in course scheduling? Are they scheduled fairly, balancing the needs of all? Elizabeth Hinson-Hasty suggests giving priority to scheduling needs of contingent faculty.[53] Trying to coordinate childcare or other work when one does not know when one will teach or when one's office hours will be is extremely stressful. Allowing contingent faculty to have greater influence when they teach and over their office hours is not just a convenience. It allows these faculty members to save funds on childcare and travel, and, while just pay is always preferred, such efforts matter. Second, it is common for summer school courses to be offered to tenure-track faculty first, then non-tenure track full-time, and then adjuncts. This may be a policy of a dean or chair. However, the option of teaching summer school allows adjuncts, already the lowest-paid and without benefits, to raise their income. Increasing opportunities to teach summer school is a band-aid approach, but it at least acknowledges a wound. Creating jobs with just pay, benefits, and stability is not just about being fair to contingent faculty, it is about institutions living their mission and ensuring they are contributing to the well-being of community.

Promoting Inclusion

While every contingent faculty member should be paid at a level that allows them and their families to flourish, they also need the material and community resources to do their job well. Part-time faculty should be introduced to other departmental faculty and the dean and participate in general orientations to the institution. Library privileges and copy services are essential as are regular and substantial access to office space (a few hours a week is not adequate). All faculty should have names on doors even when offices are shared or when a faculty member is working for only a semester. Part-time faculty should have access to assistance from departmental secretaries, if there is one, and have access to business cards, if they desire them. Not only is this critically helpful for students, it helps make the invisible adjunct visible.

All faculty should be invited to participate in departmental meetings, though participation should not be mandatory. If it is mandatory, part-time faculty should be compensated for their time. In fact, one of the most common complaints and frustrations by adjuncts and, sometimes, non-tenure-track faculty is that they are not invited or allowed to participate in departmental meetings. This seems to be rather low-

---

[52] The difference in approach could be seen in King, "Contingent Faculty and the Heart of Catholic Education," and Hinson-Hasty, "Faculty Advocate and Middle Manager."
[53] Hinson-Hasty, "Faculty Advocate and Middle Manager."

hanging fruit and a way to erode the pervasive class mentality in many departments.

Chairs are not trained in personnel management and few get leadership training, and yet they are often contingent faculty's primary, even only, point of contact with the department. Care must be taken to expand the range of contact with departmental colleagues. Foremost, I suggest that chairs and/or undergraduate advisors get to know adjunct faculty members' expertise and professional goals. Who is actively on the job market? Who intends to stay in the location due to family and community obligations? What do they want to be teaching? Do they want to be teaching in the summer? Are they most in need of benefits or higher compensation?

Tenure-track and tenured allies can make efforts to get to know contingent faculty. They can also seek out colleagues for joint projects, which would increase inclusion and provide support and encouragement for otherwise lonely work. They can make sure contingent faculty are informed about issues within the department or curriculum issues within the college. Such efforts ameliorate the spiritual burdens of being contingent faculty, and, while essential, do not replace the necessary just pay and access to benefits.

Increasing Advocacy

Advocating for contingent faculty is not a moral option; it is a moral necessity given the changed landscape of higher education and the risk to mission of Catholic universities and colleges. There are many tactics to build pressure for change. I note four: 1) advocating within one's department; 2) increasing student engagement on campus labor issues; 3) working with governance; and 4) establishing campus wide policies. Such tactics can build at least the attitude and duty of solidarity. [54]

I am thankful for and admire the courage of those tenure track faculty who have been vocal on these issues in a specifically Catholic context, notably Jim Keenan, Gerald Beyer and Joseph McCartin, as well as all those tenure line and tenured colleagues who have supported these issues at learned societies. Nonetheless, it appears to be largely contingent faculty themselves who talk about these issues. [55]

---

[54] Meghan J. Clark, *The Vision of Catholic Social Thought: The Virtue of Solidarity and the Praxis of Human Rights* (Minneapolis: Fortress Press, 2014), 107.
[55] This claim is made on my informal observation of those writing in the *Chronicle of Higher Education* and those active on these issues in the Society of Christian Ethics and American Academy of Religion. In this volume, the majority of contributors (six of nine) are contingent faculty.

Yet, tenured faculty members are in fact in the safest positions to advocate for contingent faculty. Moving towards solidarity begins in conversation with colleagues.

In addition, it is vital to affirm the credibility of "critical university studies" and for departments and provost's offices to affirm work on these issues as substantive and as work that clearly pertains to theology, religious studies, and Catholic institutions.[56] As contingent faculty members have little to no support for their scholarship, Catholic universities and colleges should count popular scholarship and service to the community as desirable accomplishments when making decisions in regards to hiring or renewing faculty contracts. Making these changes would help Catholic universities and colleges acknowledge false narratives of exceptionalism, embrace a diversity of activities and writing that count as service to the field and evangelization proper to the church.

Students hold a particularly powerful place in campus dynamics because they are the most likely to engage with other parts of the university horizontally and vertically.[57] They often know dining hall workers and janitorial staff more intimately simply because they live on campus. They are also in regular contact with their dean and other administrators. Adjunct faculty often know students better than their colleagues. More practically, as tuition-payers, they have a heightened ability to get the attention of the administration. Students have been pivotal in raising wages for direct and contract employees at Georgetown, Harvard, and the University of Miami.[58] Educating and mobilizing students is an effective strategy to protect the most economically vulnerable on campus.

Faculty, students and staff can work with governance as well. In November of 2016, United Campus Workers (UCW), an affiliate of the Communications Workers of America (CWA), in Tennessee—and therefore without collective bargaining rights and protections—successfully stopped the outsourcing of all janitorial and repair jobs across the University of Tennessee's campus system. Workers approached governance about inflated savings estimates and harmful local effects of outsourcing and faculty listened. Such successes point to the importance of functioning faculty governance that allows diverse

---

[56] Jeffrey J. Williams, "Deconstructing the Academe: The Birth of Critical University Studies," *The Chronicle of Higher Education*, February 19, 2012, www.chronicle.com/article/An-Emerging-Field-Deconstructs/130791.
[57] Wertsch, "Just Employment on University Campuses."
[58] Eisenberg, "Campus Workers' Wages: A Disgrace to Academe."

stakeholders, including community members and students, to bring issues to the attention of the faculty senate.[59]

Finally, departmental colleagues, students and governance can work together to protect the economically vulnerable on campus by establishing campus wide policies. Loyola University of New Orleans and Georgetown University have established a living wage policy.[60] Georgetown established a broad Just Employment Policy that protects the right to organize and includes an Advisory Committee on Business Practices.[61] It is not perfect. For example, the continual challenge to adjunct issues is how universities calculate the "time" involved in teaching a course. While it states that the university will "create full-time jobs when possible and part-time or temporary work only when necessary,"[62] holding administrators accountable is a harder task. Nonetheless, it is a step in the right direction.

CONCLUSION: HEALING THE BODY OF CHRIST

Meghan Clark writes, "The attitude of solidarity begins with the *descriptive* recognition of radical interdependence."[63] To begin to build solidarity on campus, it is critical to highlight how all campus workers—from faculty, to secretaries, dining hall workers and facilities workers—are all vital for the functioning of a university and demonstrate how income inequality on-campus undercuts the common good. Appreciation, while falling short of even the attitude of solidarity, at least opens the possibility of its formation. Solidarity moves to duty when each person recognizes each other person as an image of God and therefore "equality, mutuality, and reciprocity place a claim upon the human person."[64] The tactics above—providing just pay, promoting inclusion, and increasing advocacy—can begin to protect the economically vulnerable on campus. Curbing outsourcing and reducing income inequality is vital for a flourishing campus life, the moral formation of students, and most importantly for the welfare of

---

[59] See André L. Delbecq, John M. Bryson, and Andrew H. Van de Ven, "University Governance: Lessons from an Innovative Design for Collaboration," *Journal of Management Inquiry* 22, no. 4 (2013): 382-392.
[60] Loyola University Contract Committee, "Loyola New Orleans Vendor Contract Policy," *Loyola University New Orleans*, finance.loyno.edu/sites/finance.loyno.edu/files/loyola-university-new-orleans-vendor-contract-policy_5.pdf.
[61] "Just Employment Policy," *Georgetown University*, publicaffairs.georgetown.edu/acbp/just-employment-policy.html.
[62] "Just Employment Policy," *Georgetown University*.
[63] Clark, *The Vision of Catholic Social Thought*, 108.
[64] Clark, *The Vision of Catholic Social Thought*, 109.

the workers themselves. Only when we move to work for the protection of others on campus is the virtue of solidarity possible.[65]

Catholic universities and colleges have been affected by business practices that obscure the responsibility of the employer/employee relationship, responsibilities repeatedly outlined in Catholic social teaching. These are responsibilities grounded not just in what is good for the human person, or worker, but good for specific communities and humanity. I have indicated that the willingness to pay teaching staff such extraordinarily low wages has fundamentally exposed an indefensible failure of Catholic social teaching and, thus, a failure of Catholic education and Catholics themselves. These policies are undercutting the well-being of contingent faculty as employees, and, I suggest, the moral fiber and ultimately the evangelization of our institutions and departments. *Ex Corde Ecclesiae* makes this clear.

> Scientific and technological discoveries create an enormous economic and industrial growth, but they also inescapably require the correspondingly necessary *search for meaning* in order to guarantee that the new discoveries be used for the authentic good of individuals and of human society as a whole. If it is the responsibility of every University to search for such meaning, a Catholic University is called in a particular way to respond to this need: its Christian inspiration enables it to include the moral, spiritual and religious dimension in its research, and to evaluate the attainments of science and technology in the perspective of the totality of the human person. (no. 7)

This calling transcends and infuses every aspect of the institution. Catholic universities and colleges, whether in research or labor policies, must consider the totality of the human person. Thus, the mission of such universities provides, particularly in their call to tend to the whole person, powerful rhetorical tactics in the court of public opinion and, perhaps most importantly, in the ethical imagination of students.

It is easy to claim that, as in the case of climate change, there is little an individual faculty member, dean or administrator can do. Promoting a narrative of powerlessness, instead of collective transformation, is certainly less risky, less time intensive, and, frankly, less exhausting and disheartening. Perhaps it is more comforting for some chairs and some contingent faculty too. However, it does not make it ethically defensible. The current landscape of higher education demands those of us who say we love the field—and perhaps even more so those who identify as ethicists—to curb its slow erosion. Lack of action to ameliorate the burden on contingent faculty and to make

---

[65] Clark, *The Vision of Catholic Social Thought*, 111, citing *Sollicitudo Rei Socialis*, no. 38.

structural changes in institutions of higher education exploits the vocation of the profession and bankrupts the integrity of our institutional missions and departments. Pope Francis writes, "Just as the commandment 'Thou shalt not kill' sets a clear limit in order to safeguard the value of human life, today we also have to say 'thou shalt not' to an economy of exclusion and inequality. Such an economy kills" (*Evangelii Gaudium,* no. 53). Temporary and low-wage work without benefits burdens physical and psychological health and inhibits spiritual flourishing by exclusion and inequality, killing literally and spiritually persons and the full vision of Catholic higher education.

Nonetheless the potential for conversion and promise of embodying an economy of life offers a powerful remedy for the current economic landscape and for higher education. Catholic universities and colleges can be a potent form of resistance. Saying no to market rationalizations means risking anger and being ostracized from colleagues. To claim our faith at our institutions means living by and holding fast to the death and resurrection of Jesus Christ proclaimed in the Word. It means giving up a narrative of powerlessness and to accept, along with the church, "the unruly freedom of the word, which accomplishes what it wills in ways that surpass our calculations and ways of thinking" *(Evangelii Gaudium,* no. 22). Ⓜ

Adjunct Unionization on Catholic Campuses: Solidarity, Theology, and Mission

Debra Erickson

A S THE ESSAYS IN THIS SPECIAL ISSUE make clear, the ethical challenge of contingent labor in the academy is no longer a minor debate. Nor are Catholic campuses exempt from the financial pressures, market conditions, and leadership decisions that have contributed to the crisis.[1] However, the unequal and unfair treatment of adjunct faculty is of particular concern on Catholic campuses because of the commitment of Catholic institutions to the norms of solidarity, justice, community, participation, and the dignity of work embodied by Catholic social teaching. Moreover, in light of the clear teaching of Catholic ethics, the exploitation of adjunct faculty by Catholic institutions is a fact that requires not justification but explanation: how have Catholic universities come to rely on highly qualified but poorly paid instructors to carry out the essential work of the university, and why have their administrations opposed efforts by adjuncts to organize for better working conditions? Through an examination of several recent cases, this essay shows that while financial pressures may have caused the adjunct crisis on Catholic campuses, claims about mission are behind current opposition to adjunct union organizing efforts, thus pitting the institution against itself. Moreover, I draw on Catholic reflections about the idea and purpose of the university to show that this opposition is not only ethically suspect but also missionally unsound.

In this essay, I give a brief overview of recent labor movements on Catholic campuses. I then highlight academic siloing as one contribution to the continuing abuse of adjuncts before considering a specifically Catholic reason that universities have opposed adjunct unions. Next, I question this Catholic rationale by examining the role of the

---

[1] Adjunct faculty are not the only source of labor troubles for universities. Universities often contract out dining, janitorial, security services, and even residence life functions, and many of these contractors do not receive the same level of benefits or pay as regular university employees (who also may be unionized). While many of the moral arguments made on behalf of adjunct faculty apply to these groups, they are outside the focus of this article.

faculty in the mission of the Catholic university and the theology faculty in particular. I also place Catholic universities in the context of other religious institutions within the marketplace of higher education and, subsequently, draw these threads together in a discussion of money and morality in higher education. Finally, I highlight two Catholic alternatives to union campaigns and union-busting that might serve as models for other Catholic universities. The paper concludes with a coda on mission and the academic vocation. Throughout the paper, the interplay of three forces is evident: internal Catholic dialog, larger pressures in the higher education sector, and trends in the fields of religion and theology.

FACULTY LABOR MOVEMENTS ON CATHOLIC CAMPUSES

According to the Catholic Labor Network's 2018 *Gaudium et Spes* Labor Report, of the approximately 200 U.S. institutions of Catholic higher education, fewer than ten percent have faculty union representation, which is less than half the rate of all universities combined. Of the Catholic faculty unions, eight are faculty unions, eleven are adjunct faculty only, and one institution, St. Xavier, has an unaffiliated union representing tenured faculty only.[2] By way of comparison, sixteen Catholic universities are reported to be members of the Workers' Rights Consortium, which certifies fair labor practices by vendors of college-branded goods and clothing.[3] These statistics suggest a mismatch between clear Catholic teaching on the rights and dignity of workers and the labor practices of Catholic institutions of higher education that begs for an explanation.

Yet, as the one-in-ten statistic indicates, individual Catholic institutions have offered a range of responses to adjunct organizing. For instance, when Jesuit Georgetown University's adjunct faculty organized to vote on union representation, the administration remained publicly neutral on the matter, explaining its position by reference to

---

[2] Clayton Sinyai, "Gaudium et Spes Labor Report 2018," *The Catholic Labor Network*, catholiclabor.org/wp-content/uploads/2018/05/Gaudium-et-Spes-Labor-Report-2018.pdf, pages 27-33. At least one other Catholic institution with an adjunct union, Siena College (discussed below), is not on this list. Statistics on the number of universities overall with faculty unions are difficult to come by, but at least one source puts it at 35 percent of public universities and 21 percent of all universities (Andrew Hibel, interview with Timothy Reese Cain, "What Does the History of Faculty Unions Teach Us About Their Future?" *Higher Ed Jobs*, n.d., www.higheredjobs.com/HigherEdCareers/interviews.cfm?ID=315).

[3] The Catholic Labor Network, "Catholic Higher Education Institutions with Collective Bargaining," catholiclabor.org/catholic-employer-project/catholic-higher-education/.

the institutional commitments outlined in their "just employment policy."[4] The vote carried, and now many adjuncts have been converted from piecemeal employment to "half-full" contracts, granting them a measure of predictability, stability, and compensation that make a teaching career more sustainable for adjunct instructors.[5]

Other universities do not have adjunct unions but institutional policies more supportive of adjunct faculty than is typical. One example is Vincentian DePaul University, the largest Catholic university in the country, which employs many part-time faculty (according to one report, sixty percent of faculty are non-tenured). At DePaul, part-time faculty are assured of office space during the semester, given access to supplies, and paid for trainings and meetings attended in addition to their course-related duties. Moreover, the administrative elements of hiring and onboarding temporary employees have been streamlined to reduce the burden on adjuncts.[6] Amidst a union drive in 2016, DePaul established an Adjunct Faculty Task Force, and, by the fall of 2017, a new Workplace Environment Committee had been organized to address adjunct concerns.[7]

Some cited these and other outreach efforts by the administration as an attempt to prevent a successful vote for unionization, suggesting that for every positive story, a negative example is not hard to find.[8] Five years ago, Spiritan Duquesne University became briefly infamous over the dismissal and subsequent death of a long-term adjunct, Margaret Mary Vojtko, which seemed to epitomize every unethical faculty employment practice.[9] Vojtko was a loyal and dedicated mem-

---

[4] Clayton Sinyai, "Which Side are We On? Catholic Teachers and the Right to Unionize," *America*, January 19-26, 2015, www.americamagazine.org/issue/which-side-are-we.

[5] Caroline Frederickson, "There is no Excuse for how Universities Treat Adjuncts," *The Atlantic*, September 15, 2015, www.theatlantic.com/business/archive/2015/09/higher-education-college-adjunct-professor-salary/404461/.

[6] This information is taken from my own experience as adjunct faculty at DePaul University during the fall 2010 semester. To the best of my recollection, adjunct pay was about the median national average of around $2700 per course.

[7] See DePaul University Academic Affairs, "Latest News for Adjunct Faculty" Faculty Resources Page, offices.depaul.edu/academic-affairs/faculty-resources/adjunct-resources/Pages/default.aspx. As of this writing, DePaul University adjuncts have not unionized.

[8] See particularly an anonymous letter to the campus newspaper, SEIU Organizing Committee, "Adjunct Faculty Calls for Allies," *The DePaulia*, October 3, 2016, depauliaonline.com/24684/opinions/letter-adjunct-faculty-calls-allies/. Public statements by DePaul's then-president Dennis H. Holtschneider against unionization are discussed below.

[9] Coverage of the affair includes a now-famous essay by Vojtko's lawyer, Daniel Kovalik, "Death of an Adjunct," *Pittsburgh Post-Gazette*, September 18, 2013, www.post-gazette.com/opinion/Op-Ed/2013/09/18/Death-of-an-adjunct/stories/20

ber of the teaching corps, whose hours and pay were cut as she struggled with aging, failing health, family, and financial difficulties. When her story was reported by the *Pittsburgh Post-Gazette*, it quickly went viral. There is then perhaps some irony in the fact that in September 2012, one year before *l'affaire Vojtko*, Duquesne's adjuncts voted 50-9 to form a union affiliated with United Steelworkers.[10] After initially supporting the right of workers to organize, the administration did an "about-face," hiring a veteran anti-union lawyer and arguing that its character as a religious institution exempted it from National Labor Relations Board (NLRB) oversight.[11] Had Duquesne recognized the union, Vojtko's story may have ended differently.

The details of Vojtko's story were unique, but it highlights a common concern in adjunct employment: high-skill, high-investment educational labor does not provide sufficient compensation to sustain a life, let alone a family. This concern is illustrated in the case of Franciscan Siena College, which employs adjuncts in a variety of roles to manage fluctuations in enrollment and the periodic need for expertise not represented among tenure-track faculty. For many years, the college also employed faculty off the tenure track on continuing, three-fourths time contracts that paid close to parity with full-timers, but were not benefits-eligible.[12] These stable positions provided a better part-time alternative to by-the-course adjuncting. Some (but not all) of the three-fourths adjuncts received health benefits through a spouse (some of whom were also employed by Siena). However, after the Affordable Care Act passed, the college would have been mandated to provide health benefits to these three-fourths employees, which it could not afford. Thus, the positions were terminated, and the classes were re-advertised piecemeal, at a much lower per-course rate. Occupants of the three-fourths positions now faced the choice of doing the same job for less than half the pay as fully adjunct faculty or seeking other employment. While precipitated by political events rather than institutional initiative, this change appears to have been a catalyst for

---

1309180224, but also the follow-up investigation in *Slate*: L.V. Anderson, "Death of a Professor," *Slate*, November 17, 2013, www.slate.com/articles/news_and_politics/education/2013/11/death_of_duquesne_adjunct_margaret_mary_vojtko_what_ really _happened_to_her.html.

[10] Clayton Sinyai, "Union Organizing Efforts Advance for Catholic University Adjunct Faculty," *America*, October 21, 2012, www.americamagazine.org/content/all-things/union-organizing-efforts-advance-catholic-university-adjunct-faculty.

[11] Clayton Sinyai, "Which Side Are We On?"

[12] I held a position as Visiting Assistant Professor at Siena College from 2012 to 2014, and some of this information reflects events that occurred while I worked there. The union campaign took place after my departure.

a successful unionization vote among adjunct faculty a few years later.[13]

The Siena College example highlights that in addition to institutional norms, universities are also subject to pressures of the wider economic and political ecosystem, as well as to what we might term "industry standards." Indeed, Siena College might serve as an object lesson in the wider ecology of higher education: as a tuition-driven liberal arts institution in upstate New York, it must contend with a shrinking revenue base caused not only by a national decline in the college-age student population, but also with a shift in student preference away from northeastern institutions in favor of warmer climates and larger institutions with deep enough pockets to win at the amenities game. As an institution with strong local ties, Siena's excellent regional reputation is no longer sufficient, as it once was, to ensure its long-term survival. Siena, and many institutions like it, must fight for a place in national rankings, while the Ivies and their peers draw not only from their traditional pool of Northeastern prep schools but also from the global moneyed elite. In this climate, many small institutions are unlikely to survive, and, as budgets and horizons contract, the economic pressure and workloads of faculty, particularly contingent faculty, continue. This compression occurs even though the salaries of top administrators—including at Catholic universities—have skyrocketed.[14]

SILOS AS BARRIERS TO SOLIDARITY

The recent history of faculty labor organizing partly explains why Catholic institutions have opposed unionization drives by contingent faculty.[15] Though the stated reasons are both financial and missional, given just how exploitative much adjunct employment is, financial reasons are the likely drivers. Considering the service-based missions of most Catholic institutions, why do not more institutional leaders express something akin to DePaul's recognition that adjuncts are an essential—even necessary—part of the university, and valued colleagues in carrying out the institution's mission? Why have so many

---

[13] Bethany Bump, "Siena Faculty Contracts Include Better Wages, Job Security," *Times Union*, September 8, 2017, www.timesunion.com/news/article/Siena-faculty-contracts-include-better-wages-job-12183787.php.

[14] Michael J. O'Laughlin, "The Highest-Paid Catholic College Presidents," *America*, December 15, 2017, www.americamagazine.org/politics-society/2017/12/15/highest-paid-catholic-college-presidents. At some institutions with religious presidents, a donation equivalent to the market-rate salary of a lay president is made to the sponsoring order. While this helps sustain the mission, it does not help resist the trend towards outsized compensation for senior administrators.

[15] In "Death of a Professor," Anderson notes that, on average, adjuncts with union representation earn 25 percent more than non-represented adjuncts.

administrations failed to display basic solidarity with their co-laborers?

One possibility is the "silo mentality" that James Keenan describes in his recent book *University Ethics*.[16] Not only are hiring decisions and employment conditions for adjuncts localized, but those responsible for conducting faculty job searches and for the day-to-day supervision of contingent faculty rarely have power over adjuncts' wages, which are generally controlled by senior administrators. These senior administrators may never meet the adjuncts whose salaries they set, and department chairs who know adjuncts best generally cannot change their pay or automatically extend their contracts, even if the chairs want to do so. Moreover, the culture of individual achievement that pervades the academy means that every scholar is a "silo of one" as he or she must focus primarily on advancing his or her own research career as the only reliable means of ensuring employability. From this perspective, organizing presents both a career risk and a career impediment.

This "silo of one" mentality is therefore a significant barrier to solidarity. Anecdotally at least, many faculty (regardless of rank) are reluctant to engage in the advocacy for labor justice that solidarity demands. Rarely is there just one reason for this reluctance; a variety of explanations coexist. Faculty at smaller colleges may simply not see it as their issue, believing it is happening at big state universities but not at their own institution. Tenured faculty in general may be ignorant, oblivious, uninterested, unsympathetic, self-interested, overwhelmed, or powerless. (Although, it is increasingly hard to believe that any member of the profession is unaware of the disgraceful working conditions of many of their adjunct colleagues, particularly in cases where those colleagues were also part of their graduate school cohort, disabusing them of the idea that tenure-track jobs are awarded strictly on merit.) Non-tenured faculty may be afraid to rock the boat for fear of retaliation or harming future job prospects. At all faculty ranks, time spent in research or advocacy for contingent faculty is time taken away from other goals and responsibilities, particularly the all-important research agenda.

Alongside these pragmatic concerns, tenure-track faculty may be reluctant to see themselves as wage workers or laborers subservient to an employer rather than as a scholars whose professional output is somewhat decoupled from their institutional affiliation and obligations. Yet the idea that academics are professionals is largely a myth. According to the *Oxford English Dictionary*, a professional is defined as a person engaged in "a paid occupation, especially one that involves

---

[16] James F. Keenan, *University Ethics: How Colleges Can Build and Benefit from a Culture of Ethics* (Lanham: Rowman and Littlefield, 2015), *passim*.

prolonged training and a formal qualification." A Ph.D. is certainly prolonged training. However, for a scholar-teacher, a Ph.D. degree is neither a necessary nor sufficient credential for practicing one's profession. Many non-Ph.D. holders teach, research, and write both inside the academy and outside it, and the majority of Ph.D.-holders will never occupy a tenure-track position.[17] Moreover, the academy also has a faculty-level "back door," as persons without a Ph.D. who have distinguished themselves outside the academy are often invited back to teach, run research institutions, or administrate, often with higher rates of pay, lighter workloads, or more flexible job descriptions than those trained in traditional ways.[18]

This state of affairs is possible in part because unlike medicine, law, architecture, accounting, or engineering, there is no standardized licensing exam certifying the scholar, no professional organization that regulates employment (though some groups do advise), and no national union or board. Unlike members of other professions, a Ph.D. scholar-teacher cannot go into private practice—the "independent scholar" designation is a marginal one—and cannot generally sell the primary "products" that a Ph.D. is trained to produce—post-secondary education and academic scholarship—outside of an accrediting institution. In large measure, those with Ph.D.'s do not set their own salary rates, can only rarely change positions for a better deal, and do not have reasonable assurance of employment in the field for which they trained. This describes a career pattern far closer to the artist than to the professional, yet aspiring academics are still trained as if a professional future awaits them after they successfully complete their training. *On its own*, this state of affairs represents a grave injustice. With the mistreatment of its adjunct members, the injustice only multiplies.

The silo mentality runs straight through a profession that is already fractured, working against the development of solidarity and other attempts to address a collapse in the market for faculty employment.

---

[17] The figure that seems to come up most frequently is that 25 percent of Ph.D. graduates across all fields will end up in a tenure-track position. This is true even in the hard sciences, whose poor academic job outlook is tempered by the availability of jobs in industry for which a Ph.D. is a desired or required qualification. In English, the ratio of Ph.D.s to academic positions has been reported to be 10 to 1. The overall picture is given in the Academy Data Forum, "A Path Forward as Academic Job Market in Humanities Falters," American Academy of Arts and Sciences, n.d., www.amacad.org/content/research/dataForumEssay.aspx?i=22902.

[18] Several people have noted that adjunct hiring was once a way for institutions to get field-specific expertise that their faculty lacked. At prestigious institutions, this practice still exists in the form of the celebrity adjunct—recent examples include offers given to former Trump administration officials by Harvard and the University of Virginia—as well as in many professional schools, which often hire working professionals and practitioners. On the other hand, adjuncts with traditional academic training are often treated as disposable.

Some of these factors may be mitigated in a Catholic institution like DePaul, which endeavors to walk the talk in its treatment of adjunct faculty. However, even the pervasiveness of siloing is not a compete explanation for Catholic opposition to faculty unions, particularly adjunct unions. To understand that, we must consider further how faculty fit into the modern university.

THE *CATHOLIC* REASON FOR OPPOSING ADJUNCT UNIONS

It is clear that the unjust treatment of adjuncts violates norms of solidarity, fairness, and the dignity of work. The magisterium has consistently supported the formation of unions as a vehicle for protecting workers and realizing those values, particularly when management has taken a hostile stance towards workers.[19] In addition to promoting more equitable conditions of employment for contingent faculty, union contracts can also extend to contingent faculty something like a guarantee of academic freedom. Despite many universities' stated commitment to academic freedom, true academic freedom comes only with tenure—with the right not to be fired (or unhired) for just about anything short of "gross moral turpitude," as it is sometimes quaintly phrased. A union contract can also offer some of the same legally binding protections against firing for ideological reasons to non-tenured faculty as tenure does to senior faculty. As more and more contingent academics organize for unionization, Catholic universities have few morally defensible reasons not to recognize those unions.[20]

---

[19] See Michael Sean Winters, "Catholic Universities and Unions," *National Catholic Reporter*, December 15, 2015, www.ncronline.org/blogs/distinctly-catholic/catholic-universities-unions.

[20] See Dave Jamieson, "Catholic Teaching Says Support Unions. Catholic Colleges Are Fighting Them," *HuffPost*, January 13, 2016, www.huffingtonpost.com/entry/catholic-colleges-adjuncts-unions_us_56942dc0e4b09dbb4bac4f84; Michael J. O'Laughlin, "Labor Board Rules in Favor of Workers at Catholic Universities," *America*, April 13, 2017, www.americamagazine.org/faith/2017/04/13/labor-board-rules-favor-workers-catholic-universities; and Kaya Oakes, "Union Busting for God: Catholic Colleges Invoke 'Religious Freedom' to Violate Catholic Teaching," *Religion Dispatches*, June 23, 2017, religiondispatches.org/union-busting-for-god-catholic-colleges-invoke-religious-freedom-to-violate-catholic-teaching/. On the issue of "Catholic enough," see Menachem Wecker, "Can Adjunct Unions Find a Place in Catholic Higher Ed?" *National Catholic Reporter*, October 14, 2016, www.ncronline.org/news/justice/can-adjunct-unions-find-place-catholic-higher-ed:

"A key question is how religious the duties of most adjunct professors are." Wecker quotes Scott Jaschik, editor of *Inside Higher Ed*: "'If we were talking about tenured professors of theology, I suspect Seattle would prevail,' Jaschik said. 'But many adjuncts are teaching first-year composition or math, and they report that their jobs—and their desire for better pay and benefits—aren't that different at religious or secular institutions.' The desire for better pay and benefits for adjuncts comes at a time that the academic landscape has changed drastically, experts said."

However, several Catholic universities—Duquesne, Loyola Marymount, Manhattan, and Seattle among them—have argued publicly that the Constitutional guarantee of free exercise of religion prohibits oversight of adjunct faculty union drives by the NLRB. In essence, these institutions argue that they cannot be legally compelled to recognize faculty unions. These universities contend that maintaining their Catholic identity means keeping control over personnel decisions, particularly faculty hiring. In one noteworthy case, a Catholic university argued that even the unionization of its janitorial staff posed a threat to its religious identity.[21] Institutions making this case appeal not only to their mission statements but also to legal precedents. When the NLRB was established in 1935, both farmworkers and religious workers were exempted, making it difficult to impossible for those groups to gain legal recognition for their unions. Subsequently, the Supreme Court affirmed in *NLRB v. Catholic Bishop of Chicago* (1979) that the First Amendment guarantee of free exercise of religion extended to matters of hiring and firing of teachers by religious educational institutions.[22]

Given that other Catholic institutions have not opposed adjunct unionization, some critics have argued that these institutions (or their leaders) are acting in bad faith: because Catholic social teaching has long supported the rights of all workers to unionize, any opposition is uncatholic. Michael Sean Winters makes this point about Loyola University of Chicago:

> [H]ow can Loyola invoke its religious character to defend against a union organizing effort when denying the right to organize runs completely contrary to that religious character? I see that the school offers a minor in "Catholic Studies," and that they pledge to help students "[l]earn about the developing nature of Catholic beliefs and practices through history, especially Catholicism's relationship with modern Western culture and political institutions." Surely, part of that history would include the role of America's greatest churchman, Cardinal James Gibbons, in prompting Pope Leo XIII to write the encyclical *Rerum Novarum*.... Subsequent popes have reaffirmed the right to organize in equally clear terms. The U.S. bishops have stated, "No one may deny the right to organize without attacking human dignity itself."[23]

---

[21] See O'Laughlin, "Labor Board Rules in Favor."
[22] See Dennis H. Holtschneider, "Refereeing Religion?" *Inside Higher Ed*, January 28, 2016, www.insidehighered.com/views/2016/01/28/new-nlrb-standard-could-have-major-consequences-catholic-colleges-essay.
[23] Winters, "Catholic Universities & Unions."

On this account, Catholic universities' opposition to unionization is disingenuous at best, cynical institutional self-interest at worst. Moreover, universities making this argument recently have lost in court.[24]

There is one area, however, in which the religious freedom argument against faculty unionization has been successful: in the case of instructors in religion and theology. By classifying them as "religious workers," universities have a stronger legal case against unionization based on religious identity.[25] This was the case in the recent Duquesne, Loyola Chicago, and Seattle NLRB decisions.[26] These decisions narrow the anti-union precedent of *Catholic Bishop*, which extended to all faculty, and grant the government authority in determining which faculty duties entail constitutionally protected "religious activities." They also conform to an earlier 2014 NLRB ruling stating that faculty may be excluded from collective bargaining only if they occupy "a specific role in creating or maintaining the university's religious educational environment."[27] On this new, theology-exclusive interpretation, for the majority of faculty, there is no distinction between working at a Catholic university and working at a secular institution. Their teaching, research, responsibilities to students and colleagues are judged identical to that of their counterparts at non-sectarian institutions.

The issue of adjunct faculty unionization, then, leads directly to the heart of the mission and identity of a Catholic university. What does it mean to say that a university is "Catholic?" What does it mean to call a Catholic educational institution a "University?" What does it mean to be a "professor" of theology (or any other discipline)? While the Church's social teaching on unionization is clear, the answers to these questions of mission and identity are contested and shifting. Although Catholic institutions are guided by their own internal cultures, missions, charism, and theology, they are also subject to the same legal, financial, accreditation, and cultural standards as their secular and Protestant counterparts. How Catholic institutions negotiate these various demands influences, for better or worse, how they approach the issue of adjunct unionization.[28]

---

[24] See Wecker, "Can Adjunct Unions Find a Place."
[25] Oakes, "Union Busting for God."
[26] O'Laughlin, "Labor Board Rules in Favor."
[27] See Scott Jaschik, "Big Union Win," *Inside Higher Ed*, January 2, 2015, www.insidehighered.com/news/2015/01/02/nlrb-ruling-shifts-legal-ground-faculty-unions-private-colleges. However, other regional NLRB decisions have addressed all faculty.
[28] While these free exercise arguments can apply to inclusive faculty unions, union drives have primarily found purchase among the ranks of exploited contingent faculty, as tenure-line faculty at most institutions have been able to retain their pay and benefits at reasonable levels. Carroll College may be the notable exception in which the entire faculty of a Catholic institution sought union representation.

FACULTY AND THE MISSION OF CATHOLIC UNIVERSITIES

How much of a threat does the presence of union protections for theology faculty actually pose to a university's Catholic identity and mission? To answer that question, I turn to three major documents have shaped the discussion of the faculty's role in Catholic universities' identity and mission. The first, John Henry Newman's monumental *The Idea of the University*, remains widely discussed 150 years after its initial publication. Second, the documents of Vatican II, particularly *Gaudium et Spes*, sparked a new openness that led to the drafting of the brief "Statement on the Nature of the Contemporary Catholic University" (popularly known as "Land O'Lakes" or in context, simply "Lakes") by a group of lay and clergy educators spearheaded by Theodore Hesburgh, then president of the University of Notre Dame. The final document is John Paul II's *Ex Corde Ecclesiae*, which some view as an elaboration and correction of the Land O'Lakes statement.

All of these documents highlight the central role of theology in the life of a Catholic university, though with slightly different emphases. Newman, in particular, staked the claim that in a truly Catholic university, theology is the essential organizing principle of its intellectual life and in fact without it, no university can claim to be a university. This is a Thomistic epistemology undergirding a Thomistic ontology of the university: the pursuit of knowledge must be oriented to its proper end, which is knowledge of God and the world God has made. Consequently, theology should and must occupy the unifying guiding role in the activities of the university. Yet Newman was fairly pessimistic about the actual place of theology in the modern university, due in part to modern secularizing attitudes in the academy.[29] Regardless, and despite changes to the landscape of higher education since Newman's time, his account set the parameters of the subsequent debate on the nature of the Catholic university.

Perhaps in reaction to a perceived limitation of this Thomistic vision on new research, the Lakes statement declared that Catholic universities must have "true artistic and academic freedom" (1), with no "theological or philosophical imperialism" (3). It also acknowledged and welcomed the presence of non-Catholics in the university (preamble). At the same time, it acknowledged the primary importance of scholars in all parts of theology (2), and of Christian scholars in all areas of study (4), in order that the university could be the "critical intelligence of the church" (5). This was an interpretation of the passages of *Gaudium et Spes* that commend the human search for truth

---

[29] John Henry Newman, *The Idea of the University* (Oxford: Oxford University Press, 1976), part 2, sections 3-5, esp. no. 397 on pages 321-322.

within the bounds of morality and common utility (no. 60), involvement in the arts (no. 62), and direct both laypersons and academics to blend, harmonize, or bring together the teachings of theology with science (no. 61-62). As with Newman, for the authors of Lakes, the character of the university applies not only to the pursuit of knowledge, but also to the "appropriate participation by all members of the community of learners in university decisions," up to and including "basic reorganizations of structure" (10).

In Lakes, theology and theologians are still clearly essential to the life of the Catholic university, but it is not clear that they are as central as Newman envisioned. There is an impression that a Catholic university is not the standard for all who would claim true university status but rather that a Catholic university is a species of the broader category "university," which exists in both secular and religious versions (1). Noting another distinction, in an assessment of Lakes on its 50th anniversary, John Jenkins, current president of the University of Notre Dame, wrote that because of their confidence in the future of Catholic higher education, the drafters of Lakes perhaps underestimated "the difficulty of finding scholars to implement the vision[,]" and as a result "plac[ed] an enormous burden on theologians" to sustain the Catholic mission of the university, one that likely contributed to contemporary union carve-outs for theology faculty[30]

In *Ex Corde Ecclesiae*, John Paul II offered a positive vision for the Catholic university that did not fully resolve the challenges encountered by earlier thinkers. He described the university's endeavors in dialogic terms: faith and reason, gospel and culture, science and theology, Church and university, Christian and non-Christian, all engaged in the shared pursuit of truth and meaning. This is not the secular-university-plus-theology implied by Lakes. Under "The Nature of the Catholic University," John Paul II wrote, "Catholic teaching and discipline are to influence all university activities, while the freedom of each person is to be fully respected" (Part II, Article 2, no. 4). This statement echoes Newman's ideal of a universe held together by Catholic reflection, while offering a more limited and nuanced account of academic freedom than Lakes affirmed. In the section titled, "The University Community," he also emphasized the centrality of the entire faculty to the catholicity of an institution: "The identity of a Catholic university is essentially linked to the quality of its teachers and to respect for Catholic doctrine....[T]he number of non-Catholic teachers should not be allowed to constitute a majority within the institution,

---

[30] John I. Jenkins, "The Document That Changed Catholic Education Forever," *America*, July 11, 2017, www.americamagazine.org/faith/2017/07/11/document-changed-catholic-education-forever.

which is and must remain Catholic" (Part II, Article 4, nos. 1, 4). Cumulatively, the message is clear. Faculty play a key role in constituting a Catholic institution as Catholic, and the theology faculty has a distinct and irreplaceable role within the wider faculty for stewarding Catholic doctrine and ethics in a manner that is faithful to magisterial teaching (no. 19).

THE EVOLUTION OF THEOLOGY AND CATHOLIC UNIVERSITIES

At the same time as the Second Vatican Council was charting the Church's response to the changes wrought in the twentieth century, the leading lights of the academic establishment were reforming the discipline formerly known as theology into a field called religious studies. The history of the American Academy of Religion (AAR) is an instructive case. Now the world's largest association of scholars of religion, the AAR was founded in 1909 as the Association of Biblical Instructors in American Colleges and Secondary Schools. In 1922, members voted to change the name to the National Association of Biblical Instructors (acronym NABI, transliteration of the Hebrew word "prophet"). By 1933, the Association launched the *Journal of the National Association of Biblical Instructors*, changing the name to the *Journal of Bible and Religion* in 1937. Through all of these changes, the emphasis of the Association on the teaching of scripture was clear, although by 1937 some widening of subject matter is apparent. However, according to the AAR's own web site, "By 1963, the association, sparked by dramatic changes in the study of religion, was ready for another transformation. Upon the recommendation of a Self-Study Committee, NABI became the American Academy of Religion (AAR) and was incorporated under this name in 1964. Two years later, the name of the journal was changed to the *Journal of the American Academy of Religion (JAAR)*."[31] Encompassing all faiths and none, the field no longer purported to make intelligible the things of God to humankind but became instead an examination of human beings' response to intimations of transcendence, real or imagined.

Academic rigor, then, rather than orthodoxy or faithful practice, came to define the field. At many schools, formerly Christianity-centric departments of theology were reconstituted as multi-religious,

---

[31] See American Academy of Religion, "History of the American Academy of Religion," www.aarweb.org/about/history-american-academy-religion. The webpage does not mention that for many years, the AAR and the Society of Biblical Literature held their annual meetings jointly. In the early 21st century, the two associations decided to part ways and meet separately, making the AAR's transformation complete. However, subsequent leadership reversed this decision, as large numbers of members belong to both organizations. Now they meet independently but concurrently.

multi-disciplinary departments of religion or religious studies. Sometimes, this transformation was spurred on by external pressure from accrediting bodies or funding stipulations. Concomitantly, at some institutions, religious commitments came to be viewed as a hindrance to objectivity or to the pursuit of truth, while other universities sought to police the boundaries of orthodoxy by hiring only theologically acceptable faculty. In response, the American Academy of Religion attempted to make hiring practices more transparent through a raft of questions on its standard job listing form, including whether or not an institution required assent to a statement of faith, whether same-sex partner benefits were offered, and whether the institution had an explicit non-discrimination policy. While this made hiring processes fairer from the perspective of the generally progressive environment of the academy, it also functioned to shame and isolate institutions which sought to hire faculty aligned with a more traditional or sectarian Christianity.

Together, these secularizing trends changed the face of the faculty at many Catholic institutions. Fewer and fewer were led by members of religious orders and staffed by religious faculty.[32] Catholic theologians were replaced by professors from a variety of religious traditions or none. Theology departments supported the study (and therefore the maintenance and growth) of many faiths. These trends reflected shifts within the broader academy as well as Catholicism's post-Vatican II openness to the secular world, along with a desire to escape the "second-tier" reputation of much of Catholic higher education. They mirrored the evolution of Protestant institutions, small and large, many of which shed their odder sectarian practices,[33] and the opening of higher education more generally towards those formerly excluded: women, Jews, people of color, and the middle and working classes. This was also an era of growth for higher education overall: first the GI bill sent returning veterans to college *en masse*, and then the baby boom sustained higher enrollments for a generation. For a time, desires for expansion, integration, and secure faculty employment went hand-in-hand.

However, this expansion had some unintended consequences that play a role in today's debates over unionization. In at least some cases—perhaps even in a majority—the theology faculties of these

---

[32] Denise Mattson, "Faculty and Staff are the New Vincentians," *Newsline*, April 26, 2018, www.depaulnewsline.com/strategic-directions/faculty-and-staff-are-new-vincentians: "60 percent of presidents at U.S.-based member schools of the Association for Catholic Colleges and Universities are lay women and men."

[33] Some of these which I have heard are requiring women to wear pantyhose to gym class and maintaining separate sidewalks for men and women. Less odd but more widespread were required chapel attendance and prohibitions on consuming alcohol, dancing, gossip, and extramarital sex.

modernizing Catholic institutions became the last bulwark of Catholic identity amidst faculties whose members were no longer majority Catholic.[34] Even within relatively inclusive or pluralistic religious studies departments, certain positions are reserved—formally or informally—for Catholic candidates only (often through wording such as "must be familiar with the Roman Catholic moral tradition"). To paraphrase a comment made to me by one former department chair, "We'll hire a Jew or a Protestant to teach Bible, but we aren't going to hire a non-Catholic to teach moral theology."[35] While entirely reasonable from a religious identity perspective and in line with magisterial teaching, this compromise presents several ethical and missional challenges for the university which seeks to be truly Catholic in the Newman sense. These challenges are to maintaining academic freedom, the integration of theology across the curriculum, and the integrity of theology or religious studies within the university—including the catholicity of the curriculum itself.

In the first case, requiring professors of religious studies—and of ethics or moral theology in particular—to carry the weight of an institution's Catholic identity can hamper academic freedom for those members of the faculty. Even without requiring an STL or a *mandatum*, faculty who teach or write things which stretch the bounds of orthodoxy may find themselves under pressure to redirect their inquiry in a more acceptable direction. In spring 2018, Tat-siong Benny Liew, professor of New Testament at the College of the Holy Cross in Wooster, MA, found himself under fire for an essay he published in 2009 in which he applied queer theory to the gospel of John.[36] First reported in March by the conservative campus journal *Fenwick Review*, whose mission statement proclaims it a defender of "traditional Catholic principles," the story was soon picked up by major outlets including *The National Review*, *First Things*, the *Boston Herald*, and *Inside Higher Ed*, the latter of which reported both the College's defense of Liew's work and academic freedom, and President Philip L.

---

[34] While I do not have data on the current composition of faculty at Catholic universities, the stipulation in Pope John Paul II, *Ex Corde Ecclesiae*, Part II, Article 4, no. 4, noted above, that "The number of non-Catholic teachers should not be allowed to constitute a majority within the institution, which is and must remain Catholic" suggests that either some institutions had majority non-Catholic faculties or that hiring trends indicated a realistic potential for it to happen on a significant scale.

[35] Conversation with author, c. November 2012.

[36] Tat-siong Benny Liew, "Queering Closets and Perverting Desires: Cross-Examining John's Engendering and Transgendering Word Across Different Worlds," in *They Were All Together in One Place: Toward Minority Biblical Criticism*, ed. Randall C. Bailey, Tat-siong Benny Liew, and Fernando F. Segovia (Atlanta: Society of Biblical Literature, 2009), 251-288.

Borough's defense of Liew but disavowal of Liew's 2009 interpretation of John's gospel. The College's response was followed by a statement by Robert J. McManus, bishop of Worcester, MA, which questioned both Liew's work and the College's invoking of academic freedom and called on Liew to recant. As word spread, more than 14,000 people signed an online petition calling for Liew's dismissal.[37] This episode illustrates the potential minefield for religious studies scholars taking on controversial subject matter.

However, in a university setting, which presumes a commitment to the pursuit of truth discernible through reason and observation, all faculty should be free to follow academic inquiry wherever it leads, both to teach the tradition as it has been but also, following the great medieval casuists, to apply it to novel circumstances. It is difficult to teach and write with integrity, no matter the setting, if certain arguments or points of view are off the table because they are judged beyond the pale of campus orthodoxy. More to the point, the Catholic intellectual tradition has consistently maintained that there is no conflict between faith and reason, and, therefore, no honest intellectual pursuit can threaten the foundations of the faith. This should be as true in matters of theology and religion as it is in matters of biology, geology, or physics—unless theological inquiry is a fundamentally different endeavor from the other academic disciplines. And, if it *is* fundamentally distinct, it is hard to escape the conclusion that theology (and perhaps, by extension, religious studies) is not an academic discipline at all, and that it belongs in the church and not the university.

A lack of academic freedom leads to a second challenge to the Catholic university: the concentration of Catholic identity in the theology department increases the pressure on the theology or religion faculty to do the religious "work" of the whole university, the rest of which has essentially been secularized. If and when a university argues that its theology faculty should be exempt from union protections, it agrees with NLRB claims that the work of the rest of the faculty is indistinguishable from faculty work at a secular university. Consequently, unlike in Newman's vision in which theological questions were engaged across the curriculum and even set the unifying agenda for the entire university, the theology faculty simply becomes a service department, offering the same two or three required introductory courses to provide a religious gloss on undergraduates' career-prep coursework. Taken to its logical end, this approach means that, as long as a few Catholic theology faculty are maintained, the rest of the university is free to engage—or not—with the deep questions of

---

[37] Scott Jaschik, "Holy Cross Defends Professor Attacked as Blasphemous," *Inside Higher Ed*, April 2, 2018, www.insidehighered.com/new/2018/04/02/holy-cross-defends-professor-under-attack-his-writings-jesus-and-sexuality.

meaning and transcendence on which a Catholic education purportedly centers.

In the third challenge, a theology faculty that must be keepers of Catholic orthodoxy in an institution in which the rest of the faculty has full religious and academic freedom also contributes to an increasing isolation of the theology department from the rest of the faculty, as the theology faculty is *de facto* and *de jure* governed by different norms. It is in danger of becoming a vestigial and academically suspect department that is regarded as little more than a center for catechesis of mostly uninterested or unwilling students. In this role, it cannot provide intellectual leadership for a Catholic institution and is far from the ideals espoused by Newman, Lakes, or John Paul II. A Catholic institution of this sort may still officially be guided by Catholic values, but these values will lack substantive theological support or coherence. They are much more likely to sound like the social justice platform of the left or the social conservative platform of the right. Neither serves the institution or its members well. Ironically, exempting theology faculty from union protection may lead not to a *more* but to a *less* authentically Catholic institution than the alternative.

RELIGIOUS INSTITUTIONS AND THE MARKETPLACE OF HIGHER EDUCATION

As discussed so far, the current state of adjunct unionization on Catholic campuses results from the "silo mentality" that acts as a barrier to solidarity with adjunct faculty and from the grounds on which some Catholic institutions oppose faculty or adjunct unions. Moreover, Catholic opposition to unions finds strange support in a view of faculty that—in contrast to Newman, Lakes, and John Paul II—does not view them as essential to the mission of the university and makes theology faculty into a different kind of faculty altogether.

This situation is exacerbated when institutions try to maintain a distinctive, religious identity in a competitive higher education marketplace. Many mainline Protestant institutions are now either entirely secular or identify as religious only in "heritage," including some of the oldest and most prestigious American universities. Others, such as Baptist-affiliated Baylor University, have attempted to retain their religious identity even while increasing in rank and size. Still others leverage their distinctive identity for growth. In this category, the televangelist-founded, religiously and politically conservative Liberty University is the most visible. A cadre of smaller religious liberal arts colleges have managed to stay solvent, despite sailing into economic headwinds, through a combination of good leadership, loyal alumni base, distinctive programs, desirable location, denominational support, or patron largesse. Others have faced merger or closure as their only viable options.

Of the colleges that have maintained a religious identity, several have explicit faith or conduct requirements of faculty as part of an institutional commitment to the integration of faith and learning, which is usually a key aim of their degree programs.[38] Faculty members who can no longer affirm the institution's statement of belief or abide by its community standards are expected or required to tender their resignations. Others do not offer tenure, opting instead for continuing, multi-year contracts, or annual contracts signed alongside the statement of faith. In these ways, such institutions attempt to ensure not only that all faculty support—or at least do not oppose—the mission of the institution, but also that in substantive measure they believe the key doctrines of the faith to be true. At these institutions, all of the faculty are considered teachers of the faith; all are seen as integral to the religious mission of the institution.

This creedal orthodoxy approach is not without its pitfalls. In 2015, Wheaton College, considered by many the flagship evangelical institution of higher education, was in the news over a disagreement with tenured associate professor of political science Larycia Hawkins, who wore a hijab during advent as a gesture of solidarity with Muslims. Some of her public comments about her actions and the subsequent controversy that arose appeared to suggest that she held beliefs that were in conflict with the institution's stated theological commitments. The disagreement escalated and eventually resulted in her termination but not before it had become a national scandal.[39] Hawkins' story exemplifies the risks and harms of enforcing boundaries of belief and practice at the institutional level. Not every belief, practice, or person can be accommodated within an institution that exists not only to further knowledge but also to be faithful to a tradition; inclusivity has its limits. How best to protect the religious character of a university while also protecting the rights of faculty employees is not entirely clear.

---

[38] Colleges which take this approach include Wheaton College (IL), Calvin College (MI), and Westmont College (CA).

[39] Ruth Graham, "The Professor Suspended for Saying Muslims and Christians Worship One God," *The Atlantic*, December 17, 2015, www.theatlantic.com/politics/archive/2015/12/christian-college-suspend-professor/421029/. Graham notes that Wheaton also dismissed a professor for converting to Catholicism and another for issues surrounding the professor's divorce.

WHEN MONEY AND MORALITY MIX

The demands of this education marketplace make it difficult to distinguish between financial and theological reasons for institutional opposition to adjunct unionization. Three more cases illustrate this tension. In a significant 2014 ruling, the NLRB denied Pacific Lutheran University's (PLU) argument that their adjunct faculty should not be able to form a union. The university's position relied in part upon an earlier precedent, *NLRB v. Yeshiva University* (1980). In that case, the Supreme Court ruled that faculty were classified as managerial employees with significant control over the way the institution was run and therefore were exempt from union protections. For almost thirty-five years, *Yeshiva* had made it difficult for faculty at private colleges and universities (regardless of religious affiliation) to unionize. This makes the NLRB's denial of PLU's petition significant: it opened the door for full-time adjunct faculty at private institutions to be classified as workers and therefore for their organizing efforts to come under the jurisdiction of the NLRB.

Aside from creating a precedent that increased the potential for adjunct faculty union recognition at Catholic institutions, the NRLB also rejected PLU's claim that its adjuncts were religious employees and therefore exempt from NRLB oversight, a claim made despite the fact that PLU has no institutional religious requirement for either faculty or students—a fact the NRLB cited in its decision. For Catholic institutions which recruit similarly broadly, the PLU decision has significant implications for any future unionization efforts. However, the mixing of administrative and mission-oriented opposition to an adjunct union in PLU's argument, as well its claim that it paid its adjuncts better than most, suggests that PLU was simply seeking the strongest argument against unionization, rather than the most principled.

If principle was used as cover for cost-savings at PLU, the exact opposite situation occurred this past year at Catholic University of America (CUA). Faced with the same financial pressures to which nearly all universities are subject, this year administrators floated the possibility of laying off tenured professors. Called "A Proposal for Academic Renewal," the plan met with vigorous faculty opposition. Faculty responses to the proposed cuts clearly referenced Catholic social teaching: "Making cuts to faculty and staff positions while repeatedly raising administrators' salaries ... flies in the face of solidarity ... and contravenes Catholic social teaching as enunciated in key papal documents. Rebuffing multiple good-faith efforts by the faculty and staff to assist in solving the financial and academic challenges faced by the University also runs roughshod against the tenet of subsidiarity"[40] In the end, needed reductions in the faculty ranks were met through buyouts and early retirements. Nevertheless, the CUA case highlights the fact that in the modern university, faculty are merely another cost to be managed. Even if the principle of solidarity did not demand tenure-track faculty to advocate for and with contingent members of their university, pure self-interest dictates it as a counterweight to the ongoing consolidation of power by a growing managerial class of professional academic administrators—which the NLRB recognized in PLU's case as the real holders of institutional power.

While the financial reasoning is similar in both cases, on the website savecatholic.com, some faculty anonymously expressed the opinion that financial exigency was being used as a cover for ridding the faculty of tenured members deemed insufficiently Catholic: "Many of us see a connection between these [proposed] firings and the direction the university has taken in the last five years.... It certainly would facilitate President Garvey's stated goal of hiring Catholic faculty. 'We should expect Catholics to carry the ball,' he writes in a column on the university's website."[41] A direct link between the retrenchment and a doctrinal purge would be difficult to prove, but this example illustrates how funding can be used to justify mistreatment of adjunct faculty not just for financial reasons but also for theological ones.

This kind of theological and financial entanglement took an almost perverse turn at Duquesne University. The restriction of the adjunct union to non-theology faculty called into question whether there would be enough "yes" votes among the remaining adjunct pool to form a union. In other words, a large proportion of the adjuncts at Duquesne are in the theology department. This is not surprising, given that many Catholic institutions have a religion requirement for students and that even at Catholic universities, the number of religion majors is often not large enough to support a significant number of upper-division courses. When the bulk of a department's courses are introductory courses, conditions are ripe for reliance on disproportionately large numbers of adjuncts. This demonstrates again the centrality of the theological carve-out to achieving justice for adjuncts: if ad-

---

[40] See the group-authored blog post, "Save the Catholic University of America," SaveCatholic.com, savecatholic.com; See also the June 6, 2018 update, "After the Vote," SaveCatholic.com, savecatholic.com/after-the-vote/.

[41] "Follow the Money," SaveCatholic.com, May 22, 2018, savecatholic.com/follow-the-money/. The post further links this conservative turn with donations to The Catholic University of America by the Koch brothers, and suggests that these donations are influencing hiring and curriculum, citing recent revelations of Koch brothers' involvement in faculty hiring at George Mason University.

juncts in theology or religion are prevented from voting on union representation, unionization drives at Catholic institutions are less likely, perhaps much less likely, to be successful.

More worryingly, the theological exception increases the vulnerability of theology and religious studies faculty to other forms of harm and harassment, when religious studies professors may be in particular need of the protections offered through unionization. Protestant ethicist David Gushee wrote recently about a religion professor at a state institution who contacted him for advice: "Professor Alison Downie of Indiana University of Pennsylvania…described herself as the subject of a right-wing social media harassment campaign initiated by an aggrieved student against whom she had taken a disciplinary action." The student had felt "silenced" for expressing his conservative beliefs in the classroom and when chastised took to the media in protest. Professor Downie is protected by a union contract, but, writes Gushee, "The case of Professor Downie teaches many lessons, among them the disturbing one that anything a professor says or writes in any context can be used against us [sic] in a national campaign if we [sic] become somebody's target, and that targeting can quickly move from being annoying to being genuinely dangerous. All the evidence I have seen suggests that it is especially adjunct, non-tenured, female, non-white, and other relatively powerless professors who face a disproportionate amount of this kind of harassment, and that cautious administrators may not defend their faculty."[42] How much less likely a faculty member is to be defended if she is contingent, especially if there are financial ramifications.

SOLIDARITY AND MISSION

Despite all of these real and potential hazards, religious institutions are themselves a distinctive good, both for the Church and as part of an ecosystem of higher education. To maintain that good, Catholic institutions must heed the dictates of justice and solidarity toward adjunct faculty employees. Two examples illustrate what is possible when Catholic universities do this.

The first is a coda to the DePaul University unionization drive. After taking a relatively neutral stance to early efforts to organize DePaul adjuncts, then-President Dennis H. Holtschneider came out in opposition to unionization following the PLU decision, which gave the NLRB authority to determine which employees were responsible for carrying out an institution's religious mission:

---

[42] David P. Gushee, "Religion Professors Become Flashpoint in Campus Culture Wars," *Sightings*, June 7, 2018, divinity.uchicago.edu/sightings/religion-professors-become-flashpoint-campus-culture-wars.

> Crucially, for any Catholic institution, there can be no sharp division of the educational process or that institution's mission into mutually exclusive realms of religious and secular. The church's teaching, developed most powerfully by St. Thomas Aquinas and carried to the present, has always emphasized the integration of faith and reason. For a Catholic institution, as for individual Catholics, elements such as science, mathematics, service, charity, history and faith form an integrated whole that infuses all aspects of university life.
>
> Yet, in practice, the NLRB proposes to decide which of our faculty are contributing to the religious mission of the institution, with a narrowness we reject, thereby ignoring Catholic universities' explanation of the integrated function of faculty across the university.... Yet as a matter of religion, a Catholic institution must insist on the unified integrity of its teaching faculty into a single overarching mission. The faculty cannot be divided into "religious" and "secular" faculty by government fiat without impugning the Catholic mission itself.[43]

Holtschneider stepped down in 2016, stating that after achieving many of the goals set for his tenure, it was time for new leadership. In line with trends toward a smaller Vincentian presence on campus, his successor is the first lay president in DePaul's history. Many voiced concern that DePaul's Vincentian distinctives and mission were in danger of disappearing, prompting two initiatives to be included in the draft of its new strategic plan: preparing lay people to sustain the mission, where "faculty and staff are the new Vincentians," and providing leadership in the Catholic and Vincentian intellectual tradition.[44] This vision is incompatible with the theological exception of the NLRB, but, as Holtschneider noted, it is entirely consistent with solidarity and justice for adjuncts.

The second example comes from St. Catherine University, a small Catholic college in St. Paul, Minnesota. At a recent meeting of the College Theology Society, Claire Bischoff, a St. Catherine University adjunct, described how the theology department responded to a directive to cut one full-time position from their department. When the directive came, Bischoff assumed that as the newest member of the department hired, her position would be the one cut. Instead, all the members of the department gave up something—a course release, administrative task pay—so that no one lost their job. This act of solidarity avoided several alternatives that theologian Gerald Beyer says have the potential for "appropriating evil," including "accepting

---

[43] Holtschneider, "Refereeing Religion?"
[44] Mattson, "Faculty and Staff Are the New Vincentians."

lighter course loads, time for research and funding for conferences" while relying on low-paid adjuncts to pick up the slack. On Beyer's view, true solidarity is not merely refraining from union-busting; it may also require "solidarity salary cuts, if necessary, when there are real budget crises, with higher earners — including administration — giving back proportionately more."[45] Of course, if an institution's expenses continually outstrip its income, this kind of salary solidarity is only a short-term solution. However, it represents a moral alternative to the theological carve-out or pitting tenure-line faculty against adjuncts. Real solidarity can also eliminate the need for adjuncts to seek union protection, thereby preserving the independence of Catholic institutions from intrusive or improper government oversight.

There is one other option for just treatment of adjuncts that is likely both to meet the demands of Catholic social teaching *and* Catholic mission, which would also likely reduce demand for an adjunct union to levels below viability: *pay adjuncts what they ought to be paid*. If adjuncts were paid for their teaching hours as a proportion of a full-time, tenure-track assistant professor salary—that is, if a full-time, tenure-track assistant professor is paid $60,000 per annum for a 4/4 load, an adjunct should be paid $7,500 per course—and if that pay were indexed to inflation and there was a path for promotion and pro-rated benefits eligibility, adjuncts would have much less reason to pursue unionization. Moreover, good pay and benefits would attract and retain wider pool of applicants, which in turn would give universities more latitude in hiring. To date this option has not been widely pursued.

CONCLUSION

Despite the challenges and pressures facing academics and academic institutions, teaching at a Catholic university must still be considered, in some measure, a *vocation* (from the Latin *vocare*, to call). Though this term has a specific meaning in the Catholic religious context, the language has been widely adopted by laypersons across the religious spectrum to describe work that goes beyond the mere exchange of goods and services and into the realm of meaning or transcendent purpose. By referring to university teaching—particularly in theology—as a vocation, we recognize that those pursuing the vocation are responsible to something beyond themselves, which is the grounds for their pursuit. Recognizing a calling means being faithful to that calling. It means recognizing that the freedom to pursue a vocation is contingent upon fulfilling the duties of that vocation. This

---

[45] Heidi Schlumpf, "Theologians Question Catholic Universities' Use of Contingent Faculty," *National Catholic Reporter*, June 12, 2018, www.ncronline.org/news/justice/theologians-question-catholic-universities-use-contingent-faculty.

vocational way of thinking can, perhaps, provide moral justification for hiring preferentially, for seeing that sense of calling or mission a prerequisite for the job.

However, vocational language can also be dangerous. If one's teaching is a calling, pecuniary concerns are secondary, or even incidental, to the work. The most destitute of adjunct faculty are often also the most committed. They are the ones who see their work as a calling so strong that practical concerns like housing or security in old age or even health are ignored.[46] In this way, the language of vocation has contributed to the deteriorating labor situation within faculty ranks. The person who sees his or her work as a sacred calling is unlikely to walk away from it, even when prudence or justice would indicate otherwise. This person can be more easily convinced to accept higher workloads or lower pay. A sense of vocation—of doing it for a higher reward or purpose—perhaps also deters faculty from organizing to seek better working conditions.

To this distortion of calling or vocation, unionization offers a corrective. It reminds faculty that, while their labor may be a calling, they are also employees, workers in solidarity with other workers in their department, in their institution, and in their society. Unionization may not be able to return universities to the more covenantal ideal of shared or faculty governance, but it may at least prevent the worst abuses. Over the past fifty years, as Catholic universities sought to increase their academic standing, they fell subject to many of the same trends operating across higher education, including over-reliance on adjuncts and a managerial approach to education. Building a truly Catholic university is not merely a theological matter. It is a matter of re-integrating into one whole—or universe—that which has been segregated into academic silos, through actions of intellectual, economic, and human solidarity. M

---

[46] This seems to have been true in Vojtko's case, which is not an isolated incident. In 2015, *The Seattle Times* published a profile of a Seattle University adjunct whose life story was heartbreakingly similar to Vojtko's; see Danny Westneat, "Gifted Professor's 'Life of the Mind' Was also Near Destitution," *The Seattle Times*, September 25, 2015, www.seattletimes.com/seattle-news/gifted-teachers-life-of-the-mind-was-also-life-of-near-destitution/.

The Threat to Academic Freedom and the Contingent Scholar

Lincoln R. Rice

THE FUTURE OF SCHOLARSHIP IN Christian ethics is jeopardized by the predominance of contingent faculty at American universities. Over seventy percent of all higher education faculty are adjuncts, with half of the teaching faculty having part-time appointments.[1] Historian Wilfred McClay believes a large part of the adjunctification of faculty began with the financial challenges faced by universities in the 1980s, in which they "began to rely more heavily on less-expensive adjunct faculty members to carry the teaching load."[2] Cathy Sandeen, chancellor of the University of Wisconsin Colleges states, "The main reason for this shift is economic. Salaries and benefits constitute 80 percent of expenses within colleges and universities. And as institutions become increasingly tuition-dependent and face pressure from students, families and elected officials to focus on affordability and student debt, managing expenses becomes key."[3] Though specific reasons for the increase in contingent faculty can be debated, the trend has continued. From 2003 to 2013, contingent faculty at public colleges granting bachelor's degrees increased from 45 to 62 percent. At private colleges granting bachelor's

---

[1] American Association of University Professors, "Background Facts on Contingent Faculty," www.aaup.org/issues/contingency/background-facts. For our purposes, contingent faculty refers to any professors teaching postsecondary education who are not tenured or on the tenure-track. Some scholars use the term alternative academics, which also includes those in administrative positions inside and outside of academia. As a rule, these positions are not protected by tenure.

[2] Wilfred McClay, "George Keller: Intellectual Whirlwind," *Chronicle of Higher Education*, November 23, 2007, www.chronicle.com/article/George-Keller-Intellectual/26941.

[3] Cathy Sandeen, "All US College Professors Deserve Academic Freedom," *Quartz*, July 1, 2015, qz.com/437194/all-us-college-professors-deserve-academic-freedom-not-just-the-privileged-few-with-tenure/.

degrees, contingent faculty increased from 52 to 60 percent.[4] This correlates with a recent study by the Government Accountability Office, which found that roughly 50 percent of courses taught at four-year public colleges were taught by contingent faculty.[5] As Jan Clausen and Eva-Maria Swidler so poignantly ask, "From a perspective that views academic freedom as the sum of the freedoms of individual faculty members, we may ask: if three-quarters of higher education faculty today are contingent, is it meaningful any longer to talk of academic freedom as a ruling principle in higher education?"[6]

This article examines threats to academic freedom faced by contingent faculty in research and in the classroom. For the contingent scholar, both areas can be easily infringed. I also insert episodes from my own life. I believe that this is warranted since I became invested in this issue when I became contingent upon graduating with a PhD in Christian Ethics from Marquette University in 2013. I also hope that the sharing of personal examples will add flesh to the statistics and other information provided. I have not only experienced the negative effects of contingency but also seen the negative impact on fellow graduates from Marquette University, peers in academic theological societies, and others in the field of Catholic theology.

In academic circles, there is often an assumption that academic freedom is something of value and should be protected. Therefore, before addressing the threats to academic freedom in research and the classroom, this article briefly examines the merits of academic freedom as a good. Since this is the *Journal of Moral Theology*, many of the arguments in this article specifically focus on the field of moral theology, but the article also includes issues that contingent scholars face in departments of theology and in the wider American university system.

ACADEMIC FREEDOM AS A GOOD FOR CHURCH AND SOCIETY

This section argues that academic freedom is a qualified good that has limits and requires responsible use. Sociologist Joshua Kim comments, "Tenure, and the academic freedom that tenure protects, is not

---

[4] Scott Jaschik, "When Colleges Rely on Adjuncts, Where Does the Money Go?" *Inside Higher Ed*, January 5, 2017, www.insidehighered.com/news/2017/01/05/study-looks-impact-adjunct-hiring-college-spending-patterns.
[5] Colleen Flaherty, "GAO Report on Non-Tenure-Track Faculty" *Inside Higher Ed*, November 21, 2017, www.insidehighered.com/quicktakes/2017/11/21/gao-report-non-tenure-track-faculty.
[6] Jan Clausen and Eva-Maria Swidler, "Academic Freedom From Below: Toward and Adjunct-Centered Struggle," *Journal of Academic Freedom* 4 (2013): 1-26, 3, www.aaup.org/JAF4/academic-freedom-below-toward-adjunct-centered-struggle#.Wk6XBzdG3IV.

a license to engage in unhelpful criticism or attacks of the institution in which the tenured academic is employed. With academic freedom comes responsibilities as well as rights, and one of those responsibilities is to act as a responsible citizen of the community in which one belongs."[7] Academic freedom run amok is ideally tempered by peer review, particularly in research. Greater difficulties for accountability are present in the classroom.[8] Academic freedom includes choosing one's area of scholarship, though this also includes the responsibility to choose a field that will ultimately serve the common good.[9]

From a Catholic perspective, Pope John Paul II's Apostolic Constitution, *Ex Corde Ecclesiae*, provided nuanced support for academic freedom. Referring to the nature of the Catholic university, he stated, "Without in any way neglecting the acquisition of useful knowledge, a Catholic University is distinguished by its free search for the whole truth about nature, man and God… without which freedom, justice and human dignity are extinguished" (no. 4). The emphasis here is on the unique role the Catholic university can play in exploring and bringing together research and insights from theology, the sciences, and other disciplines. He saw the Catholic university as having a special role in society in that "its Christian inspiration enables it to include the moral, spiritual and religious dimension in its research, and to evaluate the attainments of science and technology in the perspective of the totality of the human person… a search that is neither subordinated to nor conditioned by particular interests of any kind" (no. 7). From his perspective, academic freedom should encourage professors to pursue moral, spiritual, and religious truths without concern that their pursuit will be hampered. Qualifying his vision with the notion of the common good, John Paul II explicitly stated, "Every Catholic University…guarantees its members academic freedom, so long as the rights of the individual person and of the community are preserved within the confines of the truth and the common good" (no. 12). With regard to our particular guild of moral theologians, he added, "Theologians enjoy this same freedom so long as they are faithful to these principles and methods" (no. 29). The document aims to ensure that Catholic theologians teach within an authentically Catholic framework, explaining, "Catholic theology, taught in a manner faithful to Scripture, Tradition, and the Church's Magisterium, provides an awareness of the Gospel principles which will enrich the meaning of human life and

---

[7] Joshua Kim, "How Critical Discourse about the Future of Higher Education Gets Discouraged," *Inside Higher Ed*, October 25, 2017, www.insidehighered.com/digital-learning/blogs/limited-academic-freedom-alternative-academics.
[8] James G. Speight, *Ethics in the University* (Beverly: Scrivener Publishing, 2016), 17.
[9] Speight, *Ethics in the University*, 18.

give it a new dignity" (no. 20). There is much to unpack in this document, particularly regarding what it means to be "within the confines of the truth" when the truth is disputed. Although legitimate arguments can be made for church-sponsored colleges to fire a professor for doctrinal reasons, John Paul II clearly judged academic freedom as a good that should be protected.

To summarize, there is the concern that scholars may abuse academic freedom in ways that are harmful to the common good. In the realm of theology, there is the additional concern that scholars may hide behind academic freedom to purport heretical views that are not in line with a specific faith tradition. On the other hand, there is the danger that without academic freedom scholars simply become mouthpieces for "orthodoxy" to retain an insecure job. This mentality harms not only scholarship but prevents tough questions from being discussed in the classroom for the benefit of students. When this is the case, how will innovative ways be found to share or promote new opinions and arguments that may deepen the theological reservoir? With this question in mind, we will examine threats to academic freedom in research and the classroom.

ACADEMIC FREEDOM IN RESEARCH

Contingent professors encounter several difficulties in pursuing research with authentic academic freedom. This section not only explores obvious roadblocks such as those caused by lack of tenure protections but also the lack of resources and time in comparison to tenure-track faculty that can infringe on one's research abilities. Lack of resources can limit one's freedom just as efficiently as active censorship. Though this section largely focuses on research and publication, it also includes challenges faced by contingent faculty when disseminating their research and opinions in popular forums such as television.

To begin, contingency affects the topics one chooses to research. Certain sensitive topics in Christian ethics can only be safely navigated under the protections of tenure. The annual conference of the Society of Christian Ethics hosts small group breakfast tables where society members who have recently published books can dialogue with other members about their research. Recently, I attended one of these sessions where an author voiced opinions in his book contrary to papal teaching on sexual mores. The author, who teaches at a Catholic university, recounted being called into a meeting with the local bishop, who disapproved of the book. The author felt free to meet with the bishop, disagree with him, and let him know that he would continue to promote the ideas proposed in the book. The author still teaches at the same university, grateful for and benefiting from the academic freedom that his tenure bestows on his writing and classroom teaching.

In my own research, I have focused more on Catholic social theory and racial justice. These are topics about which I am very passionate. However, I have purposely not done research in sexual ethics because I worry that presenting my views in this contentious area of moral theology would end the already slim hopes I have of obtaining a tenure-track position. Although no studies have been performed to measure this phenomenon, I do not believe that my hesitancy to explore controversial moral issues is unique.

Another problem facing the contingent scholar is funding and resources. To begin with, adjuncts are only paid for the classes they teach. Tenured professors are paid for teaching classes, research, and administrative duties. A recent GAO study looked at pay disparities between tenure-track and contingent faculty. They discovered that "full-time and part-time non-tenure-track professors at public institutions who primarily teach are paid about 75 percent and 40 percent less per course, respectively, than their tenure-line colleagues... [When] considering teaching duties only, however, those pay disparities decreased to about 60 percent and 10 percent less per course, respectively."[10] On top of this disparity of pay, these studies did not include benefits, which most contingent faculty do not receive. Lack of funding and low pay are part of the contingent landscape that make it difficult to dedicate substantial time to research when one must teach extra classes or work an additional non-academic job to make ends meet.

Since adjuncts often have larger class sizes, teach more classes per semester than tenured faculty, and are paid less, they also have less time for research. Tenure-track faculty receive the privilege of teaching less classes and doing more research because of the increase of contingent faculty. As Clausen and Eva-Swidler aver to tenured faculty: "Your low teaching load and routine participation in the ritual remnants of shared governance are *afforded* through my exploitation and exclusion from the 'normal' process."[11]

Finally, since most granting institutions only provide funds to nonprofit institutions and will not accept applications from independent scholars, it is very difficult to apply for research grants as an adjunct, especially if your contract is from semester to semester. In addition, letterhead and business cards are generally not provided to contingent faculty, preventing them from presenting themselves professionally.

---

[10] Flaherty, "GAO Report on Non-Tenure-Track Faculty."
[11] Clausen and Eva-Swidler, "Academic Freedom From Below," 13. Emphasis in the original.

In my own situation, I am fortunate enough to have an undergraduate degree in an area other than theology. To have time for research, I stopped adjuncting and began working in my other specialty area part-time. I do not get paid as well as a full-time tenured professor, but I am paid better than most adjuncts and have more time than many adjuncts for research. The impetus for searching out a non-theology job occurred when I was notified that my two sections of Introduction to Theology, along with over twenty other sections belonging to others, were being canceled for the spring semester. Someone had overestimated how many sections were needed for the spring, and many adjuncts, including myself, were scrambling to find ways to make up the lost revenue. I had already begun preparations for these classes, time for which I was never paid and that could have been dedicated to research. Though rare, some institutions provide compensation for the classes of contingent faculty that are canceled with late notice. Colleen Flaherty documents that the University of Vermont pays part-time adjuncts five percent of the amount that they would have been paid for a canceled class. Taking into account the national average for part-time adjunct course pay, this equates to roughly $150.[12]

Even when I regularly taught as an adjunct, my university e-mail and library privileges were restricted when class was not in session. I could not access journal articles online if I was off campus until the first day of class. The only reason I could enter the library and check out books for research or class preparation before the first day of class was because alumni, like myself, were granted those privileges. This barrier has slowed down both my research and my classroom preparation. Contingency erects structural barriers that not only increase the difficulty of producing quality scholarship but also affect the quantity of scholarship. My experience of just-in-time hiring and lack of access to research and class preparation materials is not unique. As James Keenan notes, the majority of adjunct faculty are "hired within three weeks of the beginning of the semester."[13]

In addition to academic scholarship, scholars serve the common good when they share their expertise in popular media as public intellectuals. In a recent example, Lisa Durden taught communications as an adjunct at Essex Community College in Newark, New Jersey. Durden is African American and appeared on Fox News during the summer of 2017 to defend a Memorial Day event sponsored by Black Lives Matter. Black Lives Matter wanted to create a safe space for

---

[12] Flaherty, "Contracts Up Close," *Inside Higher Ed*, April 21, 2015, www.insidehighered.com/news/2015/04/21/labor-conference-panel-centers-contract-provisions-adjuncts-course-cancellation.
[13] James F. Keenan, *University Ethics* (Lanham: Rowman & Littlefield, 2015), 46.

people of color that excluded whites for this single event. For supporting the exclusion of whites from this event, Essex Community College suspended her and, after two weeks, fired her. Public pressure played an enormous role in the firing of Durden. Essex president Anthony Munroe stated that the reason for her firing was "frustration, concern, and even fear" from faculty and students over Durden's remarks. Munroe continued, "Institutions of higher learning must provide a safe space for students to explore, discuss, and debate.... Racism cannot be fought with more racism."[14] It was terribly uninformed for a university president to a define an all-black gathering as racist. This judgment betrays an ignorance that confuses racial prejudice, which any person can have for another race, with racism as a cultural reality manifested through patterns of discrimination that are institutionalized by a society. In this sense, a small group of black activists cannot cause patterns of discrimination that materially harm the lives of white Americans. Durden tried to explain this to the Fox News host but was repeatedly interrupted and bombarded with insults in which she was likened to a Nazi.[15] The most appropriate act the university could have taken in response to complaints was to defend her viewpoints or, at a minimum, to defend her academic freedom. Instead, they conceded to misinformed public pressure and have contributed to an environment in which contingent faculty know that they could be fired for expressing their views.

In the fall 2016, Nathanial Bork was an adjunct philosophy professor at the Community College of Aurora in the Denver area. He was fired one week after informing the administration that he had composed a letter for the Higher Learning Commission expressing his concern that the college had lowered curriculum standards to improve student retention and graduation rates. In response to his termination, Bork requested a faculty hearing but was denied any form of appeal. The American Association of University Professors performed their own investigation, found the college at fault, and censured the college

---

[14] Jonathan Zimmerman, "NJ Professor Fired for Fox News Comments Points to Larger Problem," *Philadelphia Inquirer*, July 7, 2017, www.philly.com/philly/opinion/commentary/no-freedom-or-security-for-adjunct-faculty-20170706.html. President Munroe's statement is available at "Statement Regarding Essex County College and Commitment to Sustaining a Diverse Learning Community," YouTube, www.youtube.com/watch?v=vJM-UsidVvk.

[15] Her interview on Fox News is at "Lisa Durden on Black Lives Matter's Right to Assemble in a Safe Space," YouTube, www.youtube.com/watch?v=_vRMnwCk-GOU.

for violating Bork's academic freedom.[16] If I am honest, college practices like the firing of Nathan Bork would have stopped me from writing this article a couple years ago. I would have been too worried how my university would have responded to me. Although the firing of contingent faculty for expressing their views is not common, it happens just often enough to persuade contingent faculty to self-censor what they teach, research, and publish.

Attacks against academic freedom do not only affect contingent faculty, but tenure-track faculty as well. The academic freedom of tenure-track faculty is being compromised by a "knowledge economy," which pressures faculty to pursue certain research and results that financially benefit the university or a university patron. This is achieved by funneling "discretionary moneys for travel, research, and scholarships...for use in designated priority areas or 'areas of strength.'"[17] Adjunct faculty do not have to worry about this ivory tower problem since one of the problems they face is a lack of access to these funds.

Nevertheless, contingent faculty have legitimate concerns regarding the infringement of their academic freedom in the research they choose and the publication, or popularization, of their research. The obstacles raised by contingent status regarding lack of time, money, and academic resources, often rob scholars of the ability to make regular contributions of original research and "sustaining creativity" in the field of moral theology.[18] The combination of a growing contingent faculty with a lack of academic freedom should concern all moral theologians. Without the protection of academic freedom for all faculty, not only is our guild being stifled but the service of theologians to church and society is obstructed.

ACADEMIC FREEDOM IN THE CLASSROOM

Academic freedom in research and the classroom are intimately connected. One can imagine that the primary concern of those parents and students who complained about the Fox News interview with Lisa Durden was that she would teach in the classroom what she expressed on Fox News. At the same time, academic freedom in the classroom is a more urgent concern for many contingent faculty because, as previously stated, most contingent faculty have less time for research because of teaching more introductory classes with more students than

---

[16] Jennifer Brown, "Community College of Aurora Censured for Violating Academic Freedom of Instructor," *Denver Post*, November 22, 2017, www.denverpost.com/2017/06/17/community-college-aurora-censured/.

[17] Margaret Thornton, "Academic Un-Freedom in the New Knowledge Economy," in *Academic Research and Researchers*, ed. Angela Brew and Lisa Lucas (Berkshire: Open University Press, 2009), 27.

[18] Steven M. Cahn, *Saints and Scamps: Ethics in Academia: 25th Anniversary Edition* (Lanham: Rowman & Littlefield Publishers, 2011), 42.

tenure-track faculty or because of time lost as they travel between the multiple colleges at which they teach.

Matthew Hertzog states that the necessity of academic freedom in the classroom dates to the fifth century B.C.E. with Plato's *Republic*, which advocated a learning environment where both teachers and students were free to converse on important topics.[19] Hertzog proposes that Plato's notion was further developed in the Middle Ages and resulted in freedom of speech, or *Lehrfreiheit*, in the German university system of the late nineteenth century. The German notion of *Lehrfreiheit* influenced the contemporary notion of tenure in the United States, leading to the composition of a landmark document for preserving academic freedom and preventing wrongful termination by the American Association of University Professors in 1915.[20] During the 1800s, American universities relied more on donors than government aid. As a result, donors exerted more influence in the selection and/or removal of professors. Nevertheless, Hertzog notes that "a de facto tenure system did exist since faculty members typically only were terminated for interfering with the religious teachings of the university."[21] Many universities adopted the principles from the 1915 statement, but there was wide variation. In 1940, the AAUP issued an updated statement, which most universities soon adopted to attract professors after World War II. The GI Bill had resulted in a flood of students entering the American university system and the need for more professors placed the professoriate in a position to dictate the terms of their employment.[22] As Hertzog notes, academic freedom in the classroom is not only to protect the professor when discussing controversial topics but also "provide students an opportunity to question theories presented to them in their classrooms."[23]

This lack of academic freedom in the classroom was exemplified in the story of a fellow adjunct moral theologian, whose Catholic theology department summoned the adjuncts to a meeting in which greater restraints were being placed on how they taught the introduction to theology class. Noticeably absent were tenure-track faculty who taught the very same course. One of the tenured professors lead-

---

[19] Matthew J. Hertzog, "The Evolution of the Protections of Tenure in Relation to Academic Freedom in the United States" (Doctoral Dissertation, Illinois State University, 2013), 1.
[20] Hertzog, "The Evolution of the Protections of Tenure," 1, 3. For a copy of the AAUP document, see "1915 Declaration of Principles on Academic Freedom and Academic Tenure," www.aaup.org/NR/rdonlyres/A6520A9D-0A9A-47B3-B550-C006B5B224E7/0/1915Declaration.pdf.
[21] Hertzog, "The Evolution of the Protections of Tenure," 5.
[22] Hertzog, "The Evolution of the Protections of Tenure," 11-12.
[23] Hertzog, "The Evolution of the Protections of Tenure," 2.

ing the session stated that greater consistency was needed in the introductory course and since agreement for this could not be reached among tenured faculty, at least some consistency in the course could be implemented through the contingent faculty. The implication was that they could not refuse without losing their contract. I will note that the ethicist continued to teach the class as she always had because the department did not put any protocols in place to police the new restraints.

The contingent faculty had been called into this meeting because the teaching methods of certain tenure-track and contingent faculty were not properly laying the theological groundwork for additional classes in theology. This story illustrates how easy it is for contingent faculty to lose academic freedom in the classroom. However, it is more than that. This story speaks to the incongruities present when tenured faculty believe they can dictate how foundational courses ought to be taught when they cannot even agree among themselves. The department did not request any input from contingent faculty, who were teaching most of the classes. This is still the case at this Catholic university. In the introduction to theology course listing for spring 2018, tenure-track faculty taught only seven of the twenty-six sections of the class. The core foundational course is essentially contracted out so that tenure-track faculty can teach the upper level classes that are more closely connected to their areas of research.

Academic freedom in the classroom includes challenging students and presenting perspectives with which they are unfamiliar. Teaching students also requires rigorous coursework and tests to measure a student's grasp of the material. However, as English professor Janet Casey notes:

> [Contingent faculty] literally cannot afford to speak their minds on the departmental or institutional levels, nor is it difficult to see why they might legitimately dread student evaluations. They are forced to curry the favor of colleagues as well as students, potentially limiting their effectiveness as teachers and contributing to grade inflation.... The free exchange of ideas among intellectuals is little more than an illusion when many faculty members operate daily under the threat of censorship.[24]

Contingent faculty jobs are more susceptible to negative feedback from challenging students than their tenure-track peers.

---

[24] Janet G. Casey, "Taking the Leap," *Inside Higher Ed*, November 21, 2011, www.insidehighered.com/views/2011/11/21/essay-responsibilities-tenure-track-faculty-address-adjunct-issues. See also Eva Swidler, "The Pernicious Silencing of the Adjunct Faculty," *Chronicle of Higher Education*, October 30, 2017, www.chronicle.com/article/The-Pernicious-Silencing-of/241601?cid=wcontentgrid_hp_2.

Eva Swidler recently proposed a narrative that should disturb Christian ethicists. She began by relating that "over two-thirds of 2016 high-school graduates in the United States at least began college."[25] And since more than seventy percent of college professors are contingent, a great percentage of our youth will receive instruction from adjunct faculty. "But if what they learn and discuss tiptoes around topics like exploitation, violence, and racism, what are they learning? That these are not important issues to think about? That these are not issues that should concern them? That these are issues to be ignored, or even swept under the rug, lest the boat be rocked?"[26] Swidler then connects this problem as injuring the proper formation of American citizens.[27] While this should concern us, a greater concern should be the malformation of Christians because of a censorship on justice issues in theology classes.

Many contingent faculty endure censorship before the first day of class, after turning in their syllabus to the department. Eva Swidler notes that "controversial authors and readings get weeded out."[28] At a recent academic theology conference, two contingent faculty shared this exact experience where they each had chairs eliminate readings from their syllabus that were deemed too controversial.

Philosopher and ethicist Steven Cahn argues for the importance of academic freedom in theology classes at universities with religious sponsorship. Where academic freedom is under attack, he sees the danger of dichotomizing academic competence and shallow creedal repetitions. Cahn states, "Where academic freedom is secure, students enter classrooms with the assurance that instructors are espousing their own beliefs, not mouthing some orthodoxy they have been programmed to repeat."[29] While most moralists are concerned about religious orthodoxy, Cahn's point can address the fears that contingent faculty face for espousing, or even discussing, opinions that are not favored or viewed as too controversial by a theology department. Contingent faculty in ethics find themselves writing and teaching on some of the most disputed topics in contemporary Christianity. Cahn rightly states that infringing on academic freedom and exercising "intellectual control over a faculty... inhibit its search for truth."[30] In any liberal arts classroom, professors hope to have entrenched discussions in which students struggle to master the material and form their own opinions.

---

[25] Swidler, "The Pernicious Silencing of the Adjunct Faculty."
[26] Swidler, "The Pernicious Silencing of the Adjunct Faculty."
[27] Swidler, "The Pernicious Silencing of the Adjunct Faculty."
[28] Swidler, "The Pernicious Silencing of the Adjunct Faculty."
[29] Cahn, *Saints and Scamps*, 4.
[30] Cahn, *Saints and Scamps*, 4.

As a PhD candidate at Marquette University, I witnessed a tenured professor offer a new undergraduate class on homosexuality that he had designed. A couple of semesters later, the Theology Department denied the same opportunity to an adjunct. The adjunct assumed it was because the class would be too controversial for an adjunct to teach. After graduating, I was fortunate to teach classes on violence and racism at Marquette University, but I also wished to teach a course that I had created on gender roles and sexuality in the world religions. Since I believed that I also would be turned down if I offered the class to Marquette University, I submitted it to the University of Wisconsin-Milwaukee, a nearby state university, and taught it there the following semester. In the right-to-work environment inhabited by adjuncts, I quickly found myself teaching at two universities to financially support myself and find my job fulfilling.

WAYS TO MOVE FORWARD

As James Keenan notes, the treatment of contingent faculty is one symptom of a larger ethical problem facing college campuses. He argues that the problem is systemic, "In other forms of professional life, we have long recognized a strong connection between the lack of a professional ethics in a particular institutional setting and the lack of an ethical consciousness in that culture."[31] Keenan refutes the notion that universities make ethical decisions based on the common assumption that intelligence and ethical behavior are connected. Keenan believes this to be an unwarranted and false assumption.[32] Intelligence does not ensure morality. Universities must regularly examine their actions in light of moral and religious insights to make assessments of current practices and create strategies for implementing and retaining a just culture.

Keeping this mind, there is no magic panacea for solving the lack of academic freedom in the lives of contingent faculty. Since universities are largely islands to themselves, different strategies should be recommended for different campuses with the hope that individual university changes build toward a culture in which the academic freedom of contingent faculty is valued and protected. Thus, this section is not suggesting one method over another nor does it offer an exhaustive list. Instead, it lists several options that could be employed or may inspire additional ideas. No matter which path is chosen, though, the path ahead will be arduous and require sacrifice.

The Delphi Project on Changing Faculty and Student Success notes four primary vehicles for enacting change: unions, faculty senate, collaboration between all faculty and administration, and actions taken

---

[31] Keenan, *University Ethics*, 4.
[32] Keenan, *University Ethics*, 28.

by the governance of a university or university system.³³ Such vehicles could provide situations more conducive to academic freedom, such as shared governance with adjuncts, multi-year contracts, promotions, seniority preference for rehiring of adjuncts, paid sabbatical leave, grievance procedures, funds for professional development and conferences, and equitable pay and benefits.³⁴

One example of the unionization of contingent faculty for protecting academic freedom occurred at California State Polytechnic University in Pomona. Certain rights were secured for contingent faculty on campus with a contract in 1983. The initial contract negotiated a grievance policy, healthcare, and retirement benefits. It did not solve all problems, but it provided a foundation for working toward a just environment for contingent faculty. In 2002, the new contract added "longer-term secure appointments with a higher time base (higher percentage of the full-time load), annual and three-year contracts with entitlements with a certain number of teaching units, assign work based on faculty members' evaluations and qualifications."³⁵ An additional benefit enjoyed by unionized contingent faculty is community connections. If the time to strike or apply pressure to the administration does occur, connections with other union members in various trades in the area can be a great asset.³⁶ The job security afforded by unions aids contingent faculty in making commitments to academic organizations like the Catholic Theological Society of America and the Society of Christian Ethics (SCE). To use the example of the SCE, which meets every January: concurrent session proposals need to be submitted by mid-March, which requires contingent faculty to commit to attending the conference the following January even though their employment status may vary from semester to semester. Although unions have been helpful in promoting academic freedom on many college campuses, not all states protect the rights of workers to unionize.

University faculty handbooks may already guarantee contingent faculty rights that they are not aware of or are not being enforced. If the handbook does not promote academic freedom for adjuncts, pushing for the revision of an outdated handbook can be a pressure point

---

³³ The Delphi Project, "The Path to Change: Villanova University," www.thechangingfaculty.org/uploads/9/1/4/8/91481016/villanova-university_path.pdf.

³⁴ The Delphi Project, "The Path to Change: Villanova University."; The Delphi Project, "California State Polytechnic University," pullias.usc.edu/wp-content/uploads/2013/07/CAL-Poly-Pomona_PATH.pdf; The Delphi Project, "Mountain College," pullias.usc.edu/wp-content/uploads/2013/07/Mountain-College_PATH.pdf.

³⁵ The Delphi Project, "The Path to Change: California State Polytechnic University, Pomona," www.thechangingfaculty.org/uploads/9/1/4/8/91481016/cal-poly-pomona_path.pdf.

³⁶ The Delphi Project, "The Path to Change: California State Polytechnic University, Pomona."

for moving forward the discussion on academic freedom for contingent faculty.[37] Villanova University has gone a step further in creating an Adjunct Faculty Handbook that is forty-nine pages. The section on academic freedom succinctly avers what is protected and what is not: "All faculty members (tenured, tenure-track, non-tenure-track full-time, or part-time adjunct) are entitled to full academic freedom in teaching, in research, and in disseminating the products of their scholarship."[38] It also states that "scholarly discourse on religious matters is protected," but discussion of controversial topics in the classroom or in public that are not related to one's field or the "espousal of propositions that lack any scholarly support" are not protected.[39] Some scholars may not view the conditions as ideal, but they do clearly explicate which kinds of scholarship and speech will be protected. Moreover, they plainly protect the academic freedom of contingent faculty.

In 2007, the American Federation of Teachers published a document on academic freedom for all faculty. They proposed the following solutions not only to stop the erosion of academic freedom but expand its realm: (1) create dialogue about this topic on college campuses between tenured and contingent faculty, (2) have faculty hold meetings with legislators and the larger community to explain the importance of academic freedom and the role it plays in protecting a democratic society, (3) have faculty organize and negotiate collective bargaining agreements, since current tenure practices and academic freedom are mostly controlled by the college administration. This last point may also require political pressure to provide collective bargaining or similar measures in areas where they do not exist.[40]

The discussion of academic freedom on campus does not guarantee improvement. In September 2015, John Hopkins University published an official statement on academic freedom. Because the university allowed comments on the final draft, it is available for comparison with the official statement. The official statement deleted from the draft the following sentence: "Although tenure may form its backbone, Academic Freedom extends to all faculty, students, and staff alike."[41] Although the finished document promotes academic freedom, it does not

---

[37] The Delphi Project, "The Path to Change: Villanova University."
[38] Villanova University, Office of Provost, "Adjunct Faculty Handbook," November 22, 2016, p. 14, www1.villanova.edu/content/dam/villanova/provost/Adjunct%20Faculty%20Handbook.pdf.
[39] Villanova University, "Adjunct Faculty Handbook," 14.
[40] American Federation of Teachers, "Academic Freedom in the 21st-Century College and University," 16-18, www.aft.org/sites/default/files/academicfreedomstatement0907.pdf.
[41] For a copy of the final draft, see Stephen Downes, "Johns Hopkins Academic Freedom Statement – An Analytical Representation," www.downes.ca/cgi-bin/page.cgi?post=64647.

explicitly mention who is protected by academic freedom, and this resulted in a diluted document that does nothing to protect the most vulnerable members of the academic community on campus.[42]

Janet Casey taught as an English adjunct for fifteen years before receiving a tenure track position. She challenges her fellow tenure-track faculty to accept sacrifices to create a university climate that is more just for contingent faculty: "[Tenured faculty] will inevitably have to give something up. All the hand-wringing in the world will not compensate for the genuine material sacrifices—of dollars or of pet projects—that TT [tenure-track] faculty must make in order to create a faculty labor system that is more ethical and more genuinely reflective of our stated goals and priorities."[43] A stunning example of this occurred around 2013 at Clarke University in Dubuque, Iowa. The senate faculty voted to forgo their raises and instead redirect the funds to adjunct faculty. This raised adjunct pay from about $2,100 per class to $2,700.[44] This represented a 28.6 percent raise for adjuncts who had not seen their pay increase for years.

Although in the earlier examples of adjunct faculty being terminated, the professors were told the reason for their termination, most adjuncts do not need to be given a reason for their termination as they are at-will employees. Additionally, there have been instances of contingent faculty being fired based on a student complaint that was not investigated. To combat this problem, the AAUP has recommended that schools that are choosing to either terminate or not renew the contract of an adjunct "should tell instructors why they were not rehired and give them a formal opportunity to appeal the decision."[45]

CONCLUSION

Although this article has focused on academic freedom in research and the classroom as separate topics, they are connected. Cahn argues that participation in research and scholarship is a way of confirming that a professor's "skills remain at the level necessary for the proper

---

[42] See the official statement at "Academic Freedom at Johns Hopkins," web.jhu.edu/administration/provost/initiatives/academicfreedom/AcademicFreedomatJohnsHopkins.pdf.
[43] Casey, "Taking the Leap."
[44] Brenna Cussen Anglada, E-mail correspondence with author, December 20, 2017. Anglada was an adjunct at Clarke University when this happened.
[45] Robin Wilson, "Adjuncts Fight Back Over Academic Freedom," *Chronicle of Higher Education*, October 3, 2008, www.chronicle.com/article/Adjuncts-Fight-Back-Over/22742. James Keenan also addresses the lack of due process in the firing or elimination of adjunct positions and advocates the introduction of due process rights. Keenan, *University Ethics*, 48.

fulfilment of... [teaching] duties"[46] and that one still has the "intellectual rigor" to teach relevant information to one's students.[47] Similarly, Rev. Joseph Koterski argues, "The kind of intellectual formation that students may rightly expect to find at the university level will be more likely to occur when their instructors are personally engaged in research, so that what teachers impart is a personal sense of the quest and not just a set of pre-packaged results."[48] Alternately, teaching helps professors to ground their research in relevant questions since students want to understand how the knowledge of one class fits into other knowledge they are acquiring.[49] In this way, the classroom brings the scholar in touch with the questions and concerns of everyday Christians and society at large. Of course, there is the danger in assuming that one's classroom is representative of society. For example, blacks and Hispanics continue to be underrepresented at America's top colleges.[50] So their concerns are not proportionately represented in what are considered America's most prestigious institutions of higher education. Though even if professors dedicate equal time to research and teaching, Keenan cites examples of researchers at universities who are "out of touch with their students."[51] So, while there can be a mutual benefit between research and teaching, professors can utilize this benefit only when academic freedom is protected in both research and the classroom.

Though it is outside the scope of this article, Karen Peterson-Iyer rightly notes that women are disproportionately contingent compared to their male peers.[52] It logically follows that these women will not be able to present papers or publish articles as often as their male tenure-track peers. Creating pathways for the involvement of contingent scholars in academic associations and peer-reviewed publications will ensure that their voices and experiences are not silenced.

The purpose of academic freedom is not for individuals to explore personal whims but "to impart what is knowable in a given discipline, and to contribute to the development of maturity in body and mind,

---

[46] Cahn, *Saints and Scamps*, 42.
[47] Cahn, *Saints and Scamps*, 72.
[48] Joseph W. Koterski, "Taking a Catholic View on Academic Freedom," *The Cardinal Newman Society*, July 20, 2017, cardinalnewmansociety.org/taking-catholic-view-academic-freedom/.
[49] Koterski, "Taking a Catholic View on Academic Freedom."
[50] Jeremy Ashkenas, Haeyoun Park, and Adam Pearce, "Even with Affirmative Action, Blacks and Hispanics are More Underrepresented at Top Colleges than 35 Years Ago," *New York Times*, August 20, 2017, www.nytimes.com/interactive/2017/08/24/us/affirmative-action.html.
[51] Keenan, *University Ethics*, 42-43.
[52] Karen Peterson-Iyer, "Gender Justice and Academic Contingency," Presented at Society of Christian Ethics Conference, Portland, OR, January 4, 2018.

heart and spirit."[53] In this sense, academic freedom should not only be at the service of students but for the common good.[54] Contingent faculty must often make sacrifices in either the classroom or research, which makes it difficult to be an engaged scholar. As the percentage of contingent faculty continues to grow and tenured faculty shrinks, what will the future of our discipline look like? How will rigor in the classroom be affected? When will university administrators, faculty, and students prioritize the need for academic freedom in higher education? Or will academic freedom completely disappear from the realm of the university in the coming years? Although these are questions for the future of Christian ethicists in general, they are questions already facing contingent faculty. M

---

[53] Koterski, "Taking a Catholic View on Academic Freedom."
[54] Koterski, "Taking a Catholic View on Academic Freedom."

Contingency, Gender, and the Academic Table

Karen Peterson-Iyer

"We in the first world ... are responsible for ourselves—for seeing the limits of our own vision and for rectifying the damage caused by the arrogant violation of those limits." –Sharon Welch[1]

IN TODAY'S ACADEMIC WORLD of postmodern awareness, it is almost a truism to say that *where we stand* determines *what we see*. Indeed, those of us who make ethics our life's work will recognize here the Brazilian liberation theologian Hugo Assman's concept of the "epistemological privilege of the poor"—in other words, those on the "bottom of the heap," socially speaking, generally have a clearer view of reality than those at the top. Even if we aren't willing to go this far, most of us in ethics these days must be willing to acknowledge the limits of our own field of vision—that our *situatedness*, especially when we are situated in positions of relative power, can dim our insight into important truths about human experience, both individual and social. In fact, it is partly because of this limitation that diversity, in all its messiness, becomes so indispensable. Rather than sticking to a timeless and limited canon of truths, academia increasingly acknowledges that there is strength in diversity—that diversity enriches the learning community and advances knowledge and wisdom. In other words, without help and a healthy dose of humility, each of us simply *cannot* see very clearly beyond our own proverbial noses.

While the academy has only just begun, albeit imperfectly, the job of making itself more inclusive of a variety of voices, it has not done so by and large with respect to the voices of contingent faculty.[2] Contingent faculty in 2011 accounted for between two-thirds and three-

---

[1] Sharon Welch, *A Feminist Ethic of Risk* (Minneapolis: Fortress Press, 2000), 139.
[2] This tendency is beginning to be addressed by papers and studies by the American Association of University Professors, many of which are cited below. Also noteworthy is James F. Keenan's recent *University Ethics: How Colleges Can Build and Benefit from a Culture of Ethics* (Lanham: Rowman & Littlefield, 2015). In a chapter devoted entirely to adjunct faculty, Keenan does the crucial (and refreshing) work of alerting us to the deep injustices that contingent faculty face, as well as to the multiple

quarters of all instructional faculty in institutions of higher education; more recently the AAUP cite the stunning figure of 73 percent.[3] Yet these same faculty—by *far* the majority of all faculty members on our campuses—exist largely outside of the academic spotlight. They generally are paid among the lowest wages on campus, receive diminished respect among their peers, have insufficient access to scholarly resources, lack any job security, and, importantly, have little to no say in matters of university governance and decision making. Their voices, and thus their perspectives, are systemically and practically excluded from matters of university policy. Moreover, because they enjoy no tenure and thus a weakened sense of academic freedom, it seems fair to say that their views are also effectively (albeit unintentionally) muted in the classroom. By any definition of the term, contingent faculty perspectives are *marginalized* within our academic institutions.

Our institutions themselves are hurt by this marginalization of adjunct voices. A higher percentage of contingent faculty generally means a higher faculty turnover rate. Students are thereby harmed; fewer faculty are available to meet with them and come to know them over several terms, to mentor them, lead them in independent studies, and write them letters of recommendation. Collegiality among faculty members is also compromised, with fewer opportunities for collaboration and fewer colleagues to share in the workload of advising and committee work. Departmental decision making is often carried out by the tenure-track minority, while the majority of teaching faculty must carry out visions and plans for which they gave little input. Finally, the overreliance on contingent faculty entails a dramatic compromise of academic freedom, translating into reduced creative thinking and thus diminished learning opportunities for students, since faculty without hiring security are far less likely to raise controversial perspectives or challenge the intellectual status quo.

All of this comes down to a matter of fundamental justice, but it also points toward the underlying need for departments and universities to assess *reality* accurately—reality as it is ascertained by a true

---

ways that they are excluded from full and fair participation in university life. He rightly raises the issue primarily from a perspective of solidarity, focusing on how tenure-stream faculty and administrators can and should support change.

[3] National Center for Educational Statistics, as cited by John Barnshaw and Samuel Dunietz, "Busting the Myths: 2014-15 Annual Report on the Economic Status of the Profession," *Academe*, March-April, 2015, 13. See also John W. Curtis, "The Employment Status of Instructional Staff Members in Higher Education, Fall 2011," *American Association of University Professors*, www.aaup.org/sites/default/files/files/AAUP-InstrStaff2011-April2014.pdf, Tables 11-12; and New Faculty Majority, "Facts About Adjuncts," www.newfacultymajority.info/facts-about-adjuncts/.

and broad diversity of voices and viewpoints. Our ethical vision is disturbingly compromised when we fail to recognize and amplify the voices of those unequal in power and status. Miguel de la Torre puts the matter bluntly:

> Only from the margins of power and privilege can a fuller and more comprehensive understanding of the prevailing social structures be ascertained. Not because those on the margins are more astute, but rather because they know what it means to be a marginalized person attempting to survive within a social context designed to benefit the privileged few at their expense.[4]

If part of our goal as ethicists and moral theologians is to take seriously the concrete reality of the society in which we live, it would seem that a crucial step would be to pay attention to those whose voices our social structures tend to mute.

Taking this argument into the realm of academia itself, this essay examines the marginalization of contingent voices within the academy as it intersects with the gendered nature of such contingency. My claim is that the exclusion of contingent voices from full participation in our academic institutions ultimately functions to dampen important moral perspectives, disproportionately including (though certainly not limited to) those of women. Our institutions are thus impoverished by such structures and practices. When we marginalize contingent voices from our larger university systems of governance and discussion, we sideline the perspectives of many women, thereby artificially distorting our view of reality—something that is in fact deadly to the project of ethics and the learning mission of higher education. To redress the exclusion of contingent faculty from full participation in the academy is thus a foundational matter of justice *and* impinges importantly on the integrity and adequacy of the profession—that is, of the work in which academics engage. If universities are to fulfill their mission to promote genuine learning and honestly advance critical thinking, it is imperative and urgent to redress these problems. Here, I suggest doing so both by actions taken in solidarity that improve the real well-being of contingent faculty and by challenging the often-rigid structures of academia that disadvantage contingent faculty and functionally devalue the perspectives they represent.

---

[4] Miguel de la Torre, *Doing Christian Ethics from the Margins* (Maryknoll: Orbis, 2004), 16.

CONTINGENT FACULTY AND THE EXPERIENCES THEY REPRESENT

Contingent faculty as a whole comprise a diverse group. Its ranks are filled with scholars of all racial/ethnic backgrounds, though, as in faculty composition more generally, the majority of them are white. In fact, reliable and well-interpreted statistics documenting racial/ethnic breakdown within the contingent faculty ranks are somewhat elusive. Depending upon who is included, between 67 percent and 73 percent of contingent faculty are Caucasian. However, proportional to their general representation in the faculty, white faculty are more likely to be represented among the tenured or tenure-track ranks than are faculty from black/African-American communities.[5] Therefore these black contingent faculty, of any sex, can be considered disadvantaged on intersecting fronts.

Yet, other important characteristics are also worth highlighting. First and foremost, compared with the overall faculty, contingent faculty disproportionately identify as female. As of 2008, women were ten to fifteen percent more likely to work contingently than their male academic counterparts.[6] A majority of college and university students in 2018 are female; and women now comprise over half of all new Ph.Ds.[7] Yet, women make up less than 42 percent of tenure-track faculty. In fact, as compared to males, it is substantially more likely that a newly minted female Ph.D. will join the contingent faculty ranks. Women comprise over 57 percent of those holding instructor, lecturer, and unranked positions. This figure contrasts even more markedly with the 26 percent of full professor positions (19 percent at doctoral institutions) held by women.[8] Relative to their general representation on the faculty, women hold a disproportionately large number of contingent positions of all ranks: 76.1 percent of total female faculty are

---

[5] According to the AAUP, 69.2 percent of all black/African-American instructional staff are classified as non-tenure track (excluding graduate students), compared with 60.4 percent of white instructional staff, 60.5 percent of Hispanic/Latino instructional staff, and 44.7 percent of Asian/Asian-American instructional staff. See Curtis, "Employment Status." See also AFT Higher Education, "Faculty Diversity: Promoting Racial and Ethnic Diversity in the Faculty," www.aft.org/sites/default/files/facultydiversity0310.pdf.
[6] Ashley Finley, "Women as Contingent Faculty: The Glass Wall," *On Campus with Women* 37, no. 3 (2008): 1.
[7] U.S. Department of Education, *Digest of Education Statistics* 2005 (Table 246) and 2007 (Table 258), cited in John W. Curtis, "Persistent Inequity: Gender and Academic Employment," 2011, www.aaup.org/NR/rdonlyres/08E023AB-E6D8-4DBD-99A0-24E5EB73A760/0/persistent_inequity.pdf.
[8] American Association of University Professors, "Statement of Principles on Family Responsibilities and Academic Work," www.aaup.org/report/statement-principles-family-responsibilities-and-academic-work.

in non-tenure track positions, compared with 65.9 percent of male faculty.[9] Moreover, according to a 2006 study, women are significantly less likely than men to successfully "cross over" from full-time contingent to tenure-track appointments.[10]

What we are witnessing, then, is the gradual but distinct feminization of contingent labor in institutions of higher education. Women are not absent from the academy itself, but they are disproportionately absent from specific places within academia.[11] The overrepresentation of women in non-tenure-track roles should come as no surprise when we reflect that the average age of earning a Ph.D. today is thirty four years old. Thus, a tenure clock and a pregnancy/childbearing clock often closely coincide. *Chronicle of Higher Education* writer Piper Fogg argues that many women earning their Ph.Ds. choose not to enter the tenure track because they believe it to be incompatible with a healthy family life and the demands of caring for young children. Challenging the widespread perception that academia is family-friendly, she holds, "[A]necdotal evidence suggests that many female scholars are not finding the time and flexibility they would like for other priorities. Those include raising children, caring for sick and aging parents, and accommodating a spouse's job."[12] Indeed, the concentration of women in contingent faculty positions effectively translates into an academic "mommy track," where lower pay, greater instability, and lesser respect result in enormous economic and social insecurity for those who enter it. In the context of women's general socioeconomic marginalization, this is particularly troubling. The American Association of University Professors has documented that it is significantly more difficult for women in academia to move up the job ladder if they have children, and women are generally underrepresented in leadership positions within academia, both absolutely and relative to the eligible pool of women.[13]

---

[9] American Association of University Professors, "The Employment Status of Instructional Staff, Fall 2011," Figure 6, www.aaup.org/sites/default/files/files/AAUP-InstrStaff2011-April2014.pdf.

[10] The breakdown among those who successfully make this "move" is 64.5 percent male and 35.5 percent female. See Jack H. Schuster and Martin J. Finkelstein, *The American Faculty: The Restructuring of Academic Work and Careers* (Baltimore: The Johns Hopkins University Press, 2006), 220 (table 7.10) and 222.

[11] Robert J. Hironimus-Wendt and Doreen A. Dedjoe, "Glass Ceilings and Gated Communities in Higher Education," in *Disrupting the Culture of Silence: Confronting Gender Inequality and Making Change in Higher Education*, ed. Kristine De Welde and Andi Stepnick (Sterling: Stylus Publishing, 2015), 37-54.

[12] Piper Fogg, "Family Time," *The Chronicle of Higher Education*, June 13, 2003, A10.

[13] See Curtis, "Persistent Inequity," and AAUP, "Statement of Principles." See also Francesca Dominici, Linda P. Fried, and Scott L. Zeger, "So Few Women Leaders,"

At the other end of the caregiving spectrum, the needs of aging parents also drive women, disproportionally, into the contingent ranks. An aging U.S. demographic means that eldercare is likely to constitute a major work-family issue in the twenty-first century. By 2030, over 20 percent of the population is expected to be over age 65, up from 12 percent in 2000 and only 4 percent in 1900.[14] Like childcare, unpaid eldercare in the U.S. is primarily done by women, regardless of their employment status.[15] Within academia, the few studies that have been conducted confirm that it is women who overwhelmingly bear the eldercare burden. The problem is particularly sharp in STEM fields, where women are five times more likely than men to consider leaving their jobs or finding another position because of the lack of support for their eldercare responsibilities.[16] It would seem that the reality of a rapidly aging population quickly becomes a crisis for women who struggle to build their own academic careers while also caring for older family members. Many of these women will end up stepping away from the ranks of the tenure track into more flexible positions with contingent status.

The disproportionate concentration of academic women in contingent roles is not a completely new situation, of course. Historian Eileen Schell notes that from the early days of the university, contingent faculty members were not-so-affectionately termed the "housewives of higher education," disallowed from tenure-eligible roles and therefore utilized heavily in the adjunct ranks.[17] Today, while the explicit barriers to the tenure track have fallen, the implicit ones remain, including the concentration of caregiving roles among women. That is, because women are more likely, culturally speaking, to assume the burden of domestic responsibilities, they are also more likely to suffer

---

American Association of University Professors, www.aaup.org/article/so-few-women-leaders#.WqiJW2bMyBs.

[14] See Federal Interagency Forum on Aging-Related Statistics, *Older Americans 2016: Key Indicators of Well-Being*, Table 1b, agingstats.gov/docs/LatestReport/Older-Americans-2016-Key-Indicators-of-WellBeing.pdf. See also Peggie R. Smith, "Elder Care, Gender, and Work: The Work-Family Issue of the 21st Century," *Berkeley Journal of Employment and Labor Law* 25, no. 2 (2004): 351-399.

[15] MetLife Mature Market Institute 2011, cited in Gretal Leibnitz and Briana Keafer Morrison, "The Eldercare Crisis and Implications for Women Faculty," in *Disrupting the Culture of Silence: Confronting Gender Inequality and Making Change in Higher Education*, ed. Kristine De Welde and Andi Stepnick (Sterling: Stylus Publishing, 2015), 138.

[16] Leibnitz and Morrison, "The Eldercare Crisis," 142.

[17] Cited in Caroline Fredrickson, "There Is No Excuse for How Universities Treat Adjuncts," *The Atlantic*, September 15, 2015, www.theatlantic.com/business/archive/2015/09/higher-education-college-adjunct-professor-salary/404461/?utm_source=atlfb.

from the associated professional limitations. Further, the flip side of this cultural coin is that success on the tenure track (particularly in "prestigious" positions) often depends upon a spouse who is willing and able to shoulder a greater proportion of domestic responsibilities, and more often than not, culturally speaking, that spouse is female. Hence, the "individual" achievements of tenure track faculty often depend upon the undervalued and invisible labor of others.[18]

Contrary to what one might expect, then, women in academia are far from shielded from the invisible glass ceiling. Even as private industry continues to wrestle with how to eliminate invisible hurdles disproportionately impacting women, higher education—by reputation at least—enjoys a level of flexibility that would seem to mitigate this problem. Yet, that legendary flexibility simply does not seem to translate into gender equity, as the above statistics bear out. Caregiving challenges are present even in the ostensibly creative workplace of academia. Hal Cohen sharply opines in the *New York Times*, "It would seem that a university—with its ability to allow teachers to work from home, its paid sabbatical semester and its famously liberal thinking—would be an ideal place to balance career and family. But by all accounts, the intense competition, the long hours and the unspoken expectations of the academy's traditionally male culture conspire to make it really, really hard to have a baby and be a professor."[19]

Of course, there are other motives for scholars to enter the contingent ranks besides the demands of caregiving. Some are graduate students, working simultaneously to complete their degrees, some are postdoctoral fellows actively on the national job market, and some have careers outside of the academy, teaching occasional courses on the basis of their professional expertise. However, these situations are relatively unchanging, historically speaking; they do not account for the explosion of adjunct faculty as a category over the past forty years. The reasons for that explosion are complex, extending far beyond the influx of women into academia. Yet, the two trends effectively dovetail in such a way as to exacerbate the feminization of the contingent ranks.

Sociologist Eileen E. Schell has highlighted how the "standard" academic career path is in fact modeled on an individualistic ideal that is often especially difficult to attain for women with families, particularly when their early working years are interrupted by childbearing. She writes:

---

[18] I am indebted to my colleague Debra Erickson for this insight.
[19] Hal Cohen, "The Baby Bias," *The New York Times*, August 4, 2002, www.nytimes.com/2002/08/04/education/the-baby-bias.html.

The modern academic career, which is based on the ageist and sexist ideal of unlimited mobility, puts some women at a distinct disadvantage. This ideal runs as follows: While attending graduate school, the "young" (not aging) scholar should have a supportive "wife" or partner and should be unfettered by family responsibilities so that he or she can devote all energy to full-time study. After finishing the degree, the new Ph.D. must be able to move to any part of the country to accommodate his or her first academic job. Subsequent moves to better paying, more prestigious positions are also an expected part of the climb up the academic ladder. Because so much emphasis is placed on geographic mobility, academic women with family responsibilities and/or a partner who cannot relocate come up short.[20]

So understood, women's overrepresentation within the contingent ranks of academia is heavily a matter of intersecting social, personal, and institutional challenges and missed expectations. The dramatically decreased availability of tenure-track positions in the academy can intersect with any one of these materialities to translate into contingent status in a given situation.

CONTINGENCY AND THE RHETORIC OF PERSONAL CHOICE

Such grim realities are sometimes countered with the rhetoric of choice: Do not those who *choose* caregiving responsibilities deserve the costs to their careers that they incur? In the modern era, most consider childbearing an elective matter; why should the academic workplace make special provision for this choice? In 2001 *Boston Globe* columnist Ellen Goodman described this view as follows: "The world or at least the workplace continues to regard children as a personal lifestyle choice, as if women had decided to take up sky-diving or dog breeding. You had 'em, you take care of 'em."[21] According to this view, giving special accommodation to mothers of small children in fact unfairly penalizes those *without* children. The choice to care for children is understood to be an individual one.

It almost goes without saying that this approach ignores the social dimension of childbearing and childrearing. The unpaid labor of raising healthy and well-adjusted children benefits all of society as these children grow into productive citizens themselves, contributing to the common good and sharing in social burdens. So understood, the choice to have children is simply not akin to the choice to engage in

---

[20] Eileen E. Schell, *Gypsy Academics and Mother-Teaches: Gender, Contingent Labor, and Writing Instruction* (Portsmouth: Boynton/Cook Publishers, 1995), 47-48.
[21] Ellen Goodman, "Our 'Prisoner of Love' Problem," *The Boston Globe*, May 10, 2001, A21.

an individual hobby; it is, rather, a morally weighty decision that impacts the whole of society and for which the whole of society—including employers—must take at least partial responsibility.

Even as a matter of individual decision making, the choice to care for children is conditioned by the social context in which it takes place. Caregiving work—which, in the U.S., falls primarily though not exclusively to women—is generally undervalued, under-appreciated, and underpaid. The high cost of quality daycare in the U.S. further complicates such a choice. It often makes little economic sense for one or the other spouse *not* to fulfill a primary caregiving role, unless another unpaid family member can be relied upon to do so. Again, the task most often (though not exclusively) falls to women. According to economist and journalist Anne Crittenden, men in heterosexual U.S. households typically contribute no more than 30 percent of the domestic service and childcare, by their own estimates.[22] Hence the domestic burden upon a working female spouse is enormous, exacting a large emotional, psychological, and financial toll.[23]

In the face of these social and economic stressors, choice reflects both genuine human agency *and* unjust social constraints that disproportionately (though not exclusively) affect women. The rhetoric of choice, so often used to justify the career and economic costs borne by caregivers, can in fact mask serial disadvantages that profoundly impact the academic career path. As sociologist John W. Curtis writes, "Women are not so much 'opting out' of demanding professional careers as they are 'pushed out' by a combination of unrealistic workplace expectations, public policies that provide little or no support for caregiving, and male partners who neither provide significant amounts of help with household work nor are in a position to forego their own careers."[24] Seen in this more contextual light, the reasons for entering the ranks of contingent (vs. tenure-stream) faculty appear to be far more complex than simple and rational individual choice. Rather, such choices are heavily conditioned by gendered social roles and expectations, a lack of social support for caregiving work, inflexible and structurally uncreative work environments, and an ever-tightening economic belt for all but the very rich. Indeed, when women's choices in this regard are used as cause to keep them from just treatment, in the words of Judith White, Executive Director of the HERS Leadership

---

[22] Anne Crittenden, *The Price of Motherhood* (New York: Metropolitan Books, 2001), 24.
[23] See Arlie Russell Hochschild and Anne Machung, *The Second Shift: Working Families and the Revolution at Home*, Revised Edition (New York: Penguin Books, 2012).
[24] Curtis, "Persistent Inequity," 7.

Institute, "The rhetoric of choice functions in place of outright exclusion."[25]

PARENTHOOD, WOMEN'S WELL-BEING AND CATHOLIC SOCIAL TEACHING

Moving us beyond an overly individualistic interpretation of parenthood is the collective body of Catholic social teaching regarding parenthood, children and families. From a Catholic perspective, to understand having and caring for children as purely a matter of personal choice is to *mis*understand the matter entirely. Children are not "one of the many 'things' which an individual can have or not have, according to taste, and which compete with other possibilities" but rather are gifts from God to be both welcomed and protected (*Centesimus Annus*, no. 39).[26] According to this view, articulated not only by the late John Paul II but also echoed and refined by Pope Francis, fruitful married love itself symbolizes the relational mystery of God's inner life, a love whose self-giving nature ideally gives rise to new life in the form of the family (*Amoris Laetitia*, no. 11 and 13). The family, so understood, is far from a private affair; rather, Catholic social teaching has titled it as "domestic Church" and understands it as a place where the gospel is fostered and from which it radiates—a "vital cell for transforming the world" (*Amoris Laetitia*, no. 324; see also *Evangelii Nuntiandi*, no. 71).

Parenthood in Catholic teaching is thus considered a "lofty calling," deeply connected with the well-being of both the larger church and society in general (*Gaudium et Spes*, no. 47). The magisterium routinely emphasizes the particular (though by no means exclusive) importance of the role of mothers. Stressing motherhood as a manifestation of women's particular "feminine genius," Catholic teaching has in this regard tended toward a harmful gender essentialism that relies upon binary forms of male/female complementary and an arguably static understanding of the nature of womanhood. Feminists have rightly objected that these reductionist views function practically to marginalize non-mothers and to limit the social roles and vocations available to all women.[27] In some ways, then, Catholic teaching has

---

[25] Judith White, "Excluded by Choice? Contingent Faculty and the Leadership Core," *On Campus with Women* 37, no. 3 (2008): 11.

[26] While eldercare is discussed less often in church documents, the tradition does affirm—in fact as part of the Decalogue itself—the requirement to "honor your father and mother" (Deuteronomy 5:16; see also Sirach 3:12). In John Paul II's 1999 *Letter to the Elderly*, the pope notably affirms this duty as "universally recognized" and praises families who care for their elderly; see esp. nos. 11 and 13.

[27] See *Amoris Laetitia*, no. 173; *Letter of Pope John Paul II to Women*, no. 7; and *Mulieris Dignitatem*, esp. no. 30. For a fuller discussion of Catholic social teaching in this regard, see Bridget Burke Ravizza and Karen Peterson-Iyer, "Motherhood and

contributed to, or at least failed to challenge, women's *under*valuation in the workplace—academic or otherwise.

Yet, in spite of these shortcomings, it also must be noted that other aspects of Catholic social teaching have counteracted and begun to shift away from such harmful views. Pope Francis, for instance, in *Amoris Laetitia* stresses the "equal dignity of men and women" and holds that "history is burdened by the excesses of patriarchal cultures that considered women inferior.... [W]e must ... see in the women's movement the working of the Spirit for a clearer recognition of the dignity and rights of women" (no. 54). While Pope Francis arguably does not sufficiently challenge the idealized view of womanhood that we find elsewhere in Catholic teaching, his approach overall contains a shift in the direction of recognizing the real struggles faced by families today, including the challenges engendered by unemployment and the lack of supportive social structures currently available to families (*Amoris Laetitia*, no. 25, 32).

Even more germane to the discussion of women's economic precarity, however, is the celebrated pastoral document by the U.S. Conference of Catholic Bishops, *Economic Justice for All*. Here, Catholic teaching zeroes in on the particular ways that the structure of U.S. economic life and the related lack of social services challenge the well-being of both individuals and families. The bishops recognize the economic burdens threatening so many modern families and note that "great stresses are created in family life by the way work is organized and scheduled" (*Economic Justice for All*, no. 85). They go on to call for institutional and social policies whose adequacy is measured by their impact on the strength and stability of family life:

> The long-range future of this nation is intimately linked with the well-being of families, for the family is the most basic form of human community. Efficiency and competition in the marketplace must be moderated by *greater concern for the way work schedules and compensation support or threaten the bonds between spouses and between parents and children* (*Economic Justice*, no. 93, emphasis added).

It is clear here that the well-being of families is understood not as a private affair but rather as deeply connected to the common good. Moreover, throughout this document, the bishops place a clear and undeniable priority upon structurally addressing the needs of persons and communities who find themselves economically marginalized.

In an academic context today, institutions that aspire genuinely to support human well-being and the common good—and particularly

---

Tenure: Can Catholic Universities Support Both?" *Catholic Education: A Journal of Inquiry and Practice* 8, no. 3 (2005): 311-314.

those committed to the Catholic vision described in its social teaching—are thus called to attend to the plight of contingent faculty. Not only are these faculty members subject to clear economic and social disadvantage in broader society; the fact that they are disproportionately made up of women means that it is often a commitment to family that has economically disadvantaged them in the first place. If institutions truly wish to stand by a Catholic commitment to social and economic justice, the vocation of motherhood, and the well-being of families, it is absolutely essential that they attend to the *injustices* faced by contingent faculty today. In this way, they can stand with integrity on the side of human flourishing, including the ways in which that flourishing is deeply intertwined with employees' relational needs.

CONTINGENCY AND RATIONALITY

On the whole, one might summarize the situation by recognizing that *relational* demands—for instance, caring for young children or aging parents, accommodating a spouse's career path, or caring for an ill family member—are often a major contributor to the "choice" to work contingently. In contrast, the guidance of Catholic social teaching has been to honor and dignify the importance of those relational needs, even highlighting the need for policy and institutional practice to prioritize them. Of course, it is not only Catholic social teaching that has recognized the importance of human relationality in the moral enterprise; feminist thought has also contributed to that conversation. In fact, one of the central insights articulated by feminist ethics over the past thirty years is that human beings are not simply autonomous individuals but are fundamentally relational creatures. In the words of feminist ethicist Beverly Harrison,

> Relationality is at the heart of all things…. To speak of the primacy of relationship in feminist experience, and to speak of a theology of relation…is to insist on the deep, total sociality of all things. All things cohere in each other. Nothing living is self-contained; if there were such a thing as an unrelated individual, none of us would know it.[28]

Human relationality doesn't mean that we are fundamentally unfree; rather, our freedom is situated in the context of connections that anchor us, shape us and sometimes even partially define us. To ignore this aspect of our sociality is also to repudiate an important element of what it means for human persons to flourish. We are who we are in large part because of our connectedness to others, because of the people whom we care about. Indeed, the *dis*connected nature of twenty-

---

[28] Beverly Wildung Harrison, *Making the Connections: Essays in Feminist Social Ethics*, ed. Carol S. Robb (Boston: Beacon Press, 1985), 15-16.

first century American life should increasingly trouble us and, at a minimum, should serve to caution us against disregarding the importance of our constitutive relationships.

Academia's model of the "ideal" professor—geographically flexible and unfettered by family commitments, or with an infinitely accommodating and demand-free spouse—is ill suited to a fundamentally relational understanding of human persons. In fact, it is a reasonable conclusion that it is our real, human, relational needs which occasion the lopsided entry of women into contingent faculty positions in the first place. We cannot simply ignore this fact if we are to face the contingency crisis squarely and honestly, drawing connections to the structural realities that underlie that crisis. If caregiving as a whole is undervalued in U.S. society, it is women who are disproportionately paying the price for that caregiving.

In academia, the price is high. Contingent faculty earn less—significantly less—than their tenure-track counterparts. They often do not receive basic benefits, such as health care or retirement packages. They have inferior access to scholarship support and professional development opportunities. They are generally subject to unpredictable and sometimes inhumane hiring practices. They are relatively isolated professionally, subtly (and sometimes not so subtly) disrespected and generally treated as second-rate scholars and second-class citizens. They are frequently not consulted in serious ways in departmental discussions or university governance or decision making. They are, quite literally, too often deprived of a voice at the table.

SOLIDARITY AS A MORAL RESPONSE TO CONTINGENCY

Christian ethicists have special reasons to care about these patterns. First and foremost, solidarity with the marginalized demands it. According to Crittenden, motherhood is the single biggest risk factor for poverty in old age.[29] That stunning claim bears repeating: the single biggest risk factor for poverty in old age, for women, is having children. When the structures and practices of higher education function to marginalize caregivers by way of inadvertently shuffling them into contingent roles, the academy itself—wittingly or unwittingly—becomes a contributor to women's economic precarity.

Standing up for contingent faculty and magnifying their voices thus becomes an act of solidarity. Solidarity—in the words of Pope John Paul II, "a firm and persevering determination to commit oneself to the common good"—entails both an interpersonal commitment to promote the well-being of one another and a willingness to challenge

---

[29] Crittenden, *The Price of Motherhood*, 6.

social and institutional structures that devalue and dehumanize, compromising that well-being. James Keenan, in his groundbreaking *University Ethics*, identifies solidarity as a two-way street, calling diverse and yet ultimately mutually dependent constituencies into shared pursuit of a common purpose or good. The call to solidarity, he holds, is "born out of the awareness that certain social *structures* impede the relatedness among dependent groups of persons." In the context of the contingency crisis in academia, Keenan calls for solidarity on the part of tenure-line faculty towards their adjunct colleagues—including advocating for substantive changes on their behalf, but also, importantly, "finding a way of recognizing the adjunct faculty not as outsiders, but rather as one of us."[30]

Keenan's argument here points us towards a further important insight: solidarity calls those in positions of academic power not only to advocate on behalf of their contingent faculty colleagues but also to attend to the quality of their interpersonal relationships with those colleagues. To do so is to act upon and cultivate the virtue of fidelity, that is, faithfulness to concrete, particular persons. This means, among other things, *listening* to—and amplifying—contingent voices, which are currently among the most underrepresented voices in the halls of academia. Coming from a different theological tradition, Robert McAfee Brown over a quarter-century ago called for an emphasis on listening to marginalized voices even in the academic context, writing, "Instead of stonewalling with old answers, we must truly open ourselves to hear other voices particularly (for folks like us) from the third world, and not only the third world abroad but the third world within our own community and our own university."[31] Brown, speaking primarily about the relationship between the so-called "first world" and "third world," likely did not have contingent faculty in mind when he penned these words. They nevertheless ring true to the current marginalization of contingent faculty in the academy and the need to make greater space for their voices. The germane point is that, for Brown, fresh theological and moral insights emerge primarily not from sociopolitical places of power but rather from the *periphery* of power.

Understanding solidarity to include the act of *listening* to contingent voices thus reflects a deeper ideological commitment to respect the dignity of marginalized communities—of those on this periphery. Along these lines, Mary M. Doyle Roche, drawing on the work of philosopher Elaine Scarry, has incisively argued how one's *voice* is not simply instrumental; rather, it is centrally and deeply connected to one's sense of *self*. To silence or mute particular voices is not merely

---

[30] Keenan, *University Ethics*, 54-55, emphasis added.
[31] Robert McAfee Brown, *Speaking of Christianity: Practical Compassion, Social Justice, and Other Wonders* (Louisville: Westminster/John Knox Press, 1997), 149.

a practical matter, then, but rather an action that cuts to the heart of human identity and interrelationship. In this vein, listening for underrepresented voices and narratives on the (proverbial) academic margins—voices that our institutional structures so often function to marginalize—is itself an important act in solidarity.[32] Morally speaking, a commitment to such listening serves as an invitation to our institutions—especially those claiming an ethical "mission statement" at their heart—to stand and act in genuine solidarity.

EXPERIENCE, JUSTICE, AND WHO SITS AT THE ACADEMIC TABLE

Additional reasons exist—beyond a commitment to solidarity—to make greater space for contingent faculty in conversations of governance at our institutions. The costs of these gendered patterns are borne not only by contingent faculty but also by the entire academic enterprise itself. When the voices of contingent faculty—the *vast majority* of faculty on our campuses today—are excluded from the table so are their experiences. In other words, also disproportionately excluded from the proverbial conversation are the lessons absorbed by people who have chosen to step into a caregiving role at an inopportune time; or the wisdom gained through the experience of serious, career-derailing illness; or the insights garnered by those who daily face life's challenges without the career safety-net of tenure. Excluded is the perspective of someone who, of necessity, may have stepped into a precarious or even sacrificial role in order to honor relational commitments. *And these constitute an important set of experiences in our human reality.* Thus, when the academy effectively mutes the voices of contingent faculty—the faculty that constitute its genuine "margins"—it in fact weakens *itself*. It deprives itself of these experiences, and those very experiences make up a critical source of our collective moral wisdom.

From the perspective of ethics, the role of experience is essential. In one way, experience is prior to every other source of moral wisdom, for we humans draw upon that experience—our own and that of others—both explicitly and implicitly as we discern our understanding of reality itself, not to mention our moral norms. Experience is in a sense the final arbiter for our ethical directives, the final test of the adequacy of our interpretation of the world. Yet, our experiences are not self-interpreting; they must rather be deciphered within diverse communities of trust, communities where the ideas and understandings of all present can be tested and stretched by experiences not their own. This is true not just in theology or ethics but also in many different aca-

---

[32] Mary M. Doyle Roche, "Virtues and Voices: Building Solidarity among Women Scholars," in *Women, Wisdom, and Witness*, ed. Rosemary P. Carbine and Kathleen J. Dolphin (Collegeville: Liturgical Press, 2012), 100 and 104.

demic disciplines; as theologian James Gustafson once wrote, "Experience is prior to reflection.... [It] is not only socially generated; it is socially tested. And it is experience of others, of 'things' objective to human persons. This is the case in the sciences, in ethics, and in theology; it is the case in all ways of knowing and understanding."[33]

In truth, we are unable to *know* certain things apart from experience. This is not primarily because of a willed selfishness, though in some cases it could be. It is, rather, because certain realities are structurally masked from those who have not gone through them. The "cultural myopia" that Keenan describes as characteristic of university communities in fact represents just this sort of unintentional concealment of the plight of adjunct teachers.[34] The marginalization is not because non-adjuncts are malicious people; it is because their experiences are different from those of contingent faculty, and those experiences do not ordinarily conduce to seeing with clarity the very real challenges that contingent faculty face.

At issue is *what* we know, as well as *how* we know it. There are certain truths and realities of life that we deprive ourselves of when we systemically discourage contingent voices from the tables of institutional governance and decision-making as well as from positions of power and authority, both in the classroom and in collegial conversation. These truths and lived realities become underrepresented—truths about love, sacrifice, commitment, relational intimacy, and struggle. From the perspective of the quest for knowledge, it is particularly disturbing that the threat to academic freedom posed by the contingency crisis is disproportionately concentrated among *women*. How can we, as ethicists in good conscience, profess to speak accurately about the world and the relationships that compose it, when our institutions systematically exclude these contingent voices? The answer is that we cannot.

Certainly, contingent faculty have no corner on truth, but contingent faculty *do* have a point of view that is uniquely shaped by the very circumstances that have led them to contingent positions. Frequently, these circumstances reflect deeply relational instincts and constraints. Moreover, these instincts and constraints work to challenge the atavistic paradigm of the free-floating scholar, a paradigm ill-suited to a society that professes to value relationships marked by equality and mutuality. We must begin valuing contingent faculty in

---

[33] James Gustafson, *Ethics from a Theocentric Perspective, Volume One: Theology and Ethics* (Chicago: University of Chicago Press,1981), 115. For an insightful summary of Gustafson's position, see Margaret A. Farley, "The Role of Experience in Moral Discernment," in *Changing the Questions: Explorations in Christian Ethics*, ed. Jamie L. Manson (Maryknoll: Orbis Books, 2015), 52-54.
[34] Keenan, *University Ethics*, 39-40 and Chapter 5.

part for their unique contributions, contributions that are essential to advancing our fullest understanding of what it means to be a just and wise society.

In fact, Christian feminist ethicist Margaret Farley has elaborated her understanding of justice itself in a way that is closely intertwined with the need to pay attention to this sort of diversity within human experience. Farley holds that justice—understood in its classic formal meaning, "rendering to each her or his due"—necessitates that we affirm each person according to his or her concrete reality, actual and potential.[35] Yet, reality and truth are best discerned in broadly-inclusive communities where we hold each other accountable and seek to make our experiences intelligible to one another. Farley writes, "A major part of what is at stake [when we consider experience as a source for moral discernment] is the nature of knowledge itself, its power and manner of access to reality, its cognitive and affective components, its communicability, and its consequences for those who come to know."[36] In this way, communication becomes a means of bridging disparate experiences. We both learn from each other and test our own interpretation of reality against that of others, in our quest for more accurate and complete articulations of truth.

In similar fashion, philosopher Seyla Benhabib has powerfully argued that the identification of the "moral point of view" is most accurate when it occurs along the lines of a moral conversation, where *all* are included at the proverbial table. Benhabib is eager to avoid the false universalism so common to Enlightenment thought, that is, a universalism based upon an abstract, ahistorical, and unencumbered (and usually male) ego. Rather, she seeks to retrieve the positive aspects of universalism—including universal respect for each person in virtue of their humanity, economic and social justice and equality, and democratic participation—even while attending to valid feminist, communitarian and postmodern claims that are more contextually sensitive to particularity and take better account of the narrative self.[37] Drawing on Habermas's communicative ethics, Benhabib makes a compelling case that moral justification *depends* upon the presence of equal conversational participants in this way: "The fairness of moral norms and the integrity of moral values can only be established via a process of practical argumentation, which allows its participants full equality in

---

[35] Margaret A. Farley, *Just Love: A Framework for Christian Sexual Ethics* (New York: Continuum, 2006), 208-209.
[36] Farley, "The Role of Experience," 62; see also 57 and 64-67.
[37] Seyla Benhabib, *Situating the Self* (New York: Routledge, 1992), 2-5.

initiating and continuing the debate and suggesting new subject matters for moral justification."[38] Thus, retaining crucial insights of a universalist posture, Benhabib creates space for a multiplicity of voices in the discernment of truth.

When seen in this light, diversity in our academic community itself becomes indispensable. Diversity in our time has become a buzzword of sorts, often serving merely as a tick box on the list of what makes for an ethical and just community, but it is essential to stress that diversity in fact serves the larger advancement of knowledge and wisdom and as a pathway to deeper moral insight. It does not simply serve to "cast light upon particulars" of unjust social situations but also, in the words of womanist ethicist Traci West, to offer "alternatives and challenges to what is assumed ... to be the essential terms for describing human moral behavior."[39] The way we interpret the world—both in the choice of sources that we draw upon and in the conclusions that we derive from those sources—is sorely compromised if certain categories of persons are systematically excluded from or devalued within the conversation. This is particularly true if those persons are unequal in power and social status in the broader society, and, in the case of academic faculty, such systemically marginalized persons, proportionately speaking, are more likely to be women.

REEXAMINING CONTINGENCY WITH NEW EYES

It seems accurate to conclude that both solidarity and justice require us to reassess the place of contingency in the academy, including both the treatment and status of actual contingent faculty members and their inclusion in decision-making structures. The under-remuneration and compromised job security of contingent faculty members undoubtedly contribute disproportionately to women's general economic precarity. Such treatment also belies any professed commitment to honor the work of caregiving, by women or men, since caregiving itself is a major reason that scholars may opt out (or be edged out) of the tenure track.[40] To the extent that the voices of contingent faculty are muted or absent from our "tables" of institutional governance, our universities become both *unjust* and *impoverished* places.

Many institutions committed to a faith-based self-understanding will in fact be quick to assert that they *do* seek ways to honor and

---

[38] Benhabib, *Situating the Self*, 9 and 73.
[39] Traci C. West, *Disruptive Christian Ethics: When Racism and Women's Lives Matter* (Louisville: Westminster John Knox Press, 2006), 7.
[40] For a fuller discussion of Catholic institutions' professed support for motherhood as it conflicts with actual practice vis-à-vis the professoriate, see Ravizza and Peterson-Iyer, "Motherhood and Tenure," 305-325.

respect the relational identities of their faculty. Ordinarily, this commitment plays out by way of on-campus childcare, the provision of temporary family medical leave, or, less commonly, the possibility of a delayed tenure clock—all of which are worthy and important steps. However, such benefits are often denied or irrelevant to contingent faculty and only begin to scratch the surface of a far deeper and more culturally-entrenched problem.

Part of the trouble is that, as indicated above, academia itself is patterned on the model of an essentially independent, atavistic scholar who is free of relational commitments or, alternatively, whose professional choices are backed by a partner flexibly able to support those choices. This may have been an accurate (even if practically unjust) ideal fifty years ago, in *some* communities; but it most certainly is not so now. Economic realities are such that most American families depend on the presence of at least two wage-earners. In fact, this has always been true for most non-white families. The resulting geographic inflexibility belies the myth that scholars can uproot themselves with ease, moving to wherever there happen to be "better" academic positions available at any given time. This limitation, combined with the severe curtailment over the past thirty years of tenure-stream positions in higher education overall, means that many scholars *will* find themselves restricted to contingent faculty positions. Insofar as our institutional structures continue to marginalize persons who inhabit those positions, they also deprioritize the relational commitments that distinguish those persons and that put them in those positions in the first place. As a result, "The pool of potential leaders is smaller and less rich than it could be."[41]

Ethicists and moral theologians can, and should, stand as a model for the rest of our universities in this regard. If *those directly engaged in moral deliberation* choose to remain willfully blind to these challenges and shortfalls, surely others in our institutions will easily find an excuse to do the same. If moral theologians and other ethicists can work to promote and set a more just and inclusive example, however, it will be far more difficult for administrators and other departments to avoid doing so. It is incumbent upon moral theology as a discipline, then, not only to help uncover and lay bare the systemic injustices working against contingent faculty but also to offer concrete suggestions for change.

What is to be done, then—from the perspectives of both solidarity and justice—to concretely redress the situation? First and foremost, at the heart of any changes that universities make there must be a rejection of the individualist, non-relational "universal" archetype of the

---

[41] White, "Excluded by Choice?" 11.

teacher-scholar—patterned after a single-income wage-earning male. This model does not match the reality of most modern-day scholars, and it *definitely* does not match the reality of caregiving scholars— proportionately more of whom are women. Inflexible, outdated paradigms of academic career paths, with rigid boundaries between part-time and full-time, tenure-stream and non-tenure-stream positions, are a relic from a society marked by patriarchal assumptions about a woman's role in the family and workplace. In contrast to these obsolete models, institutions today must be invited to wholeheartedly embrace flexible and creative work policies, for those both on and off the tenure-track. Further, tenure itself, rather than being understood primarily as a reward for excellence in research, should be reframed so that the work of teaching—so disproportionately concentrated now in the contingent ranks—is re-integrated into the scholarly identity at all levels.

While certainly some faculty may have opted into contingent positions, the vast majority of such faculty indicate that they would prefer tenure-track posts.[42] Thus, if the tenure system is to remain intact, a key revision necessary will be the conversion of current contingent positions into tenure-stream positions. The American Association of University Professors (AAUP) in fact promotes this very step as perhaps the best way to stabilize the faculty and serve the needs of higher education in the midst of the current contingency crisis. Importantly, such conversion of positions must be executed so as not to harm experienced, qualified faculty who currently occupy contingent roles. Hence the AAUP recommends relying primarily on attrition for the gradual reduction of the contingent ranks as institutions seek to expand the proportion of tenure-eligible positions.[43] In addition, faculty originally hired on a contingent basis should be eligible for tenure based primarily on their past experience and teaching excellence. In this way, the boundary between tenure- and non-tenure-stream positions may be understood as far more fluid and flexible than is often currently the case.

Another step that universities can take to honor and accommodate the relational commitments of scholars would be the creation of fractional tenure-eligible positions, with fully proportionate pay rates, pro-

---

[42] Finley, "Women as Contingent Faculty," 1. According to a 2012 study done by the Coalition on the Academic Workforce, only around a quarter of part-time non-tenure-track faculty prefer to work off the tenure track; the remaining three-quarters would prefer a full-time tenure-track position. See "A Portrait of Part-Time Faculty Members," 9, www.academicworkforce.org/CAW_portrait_2012.pdf.

[43] American Association of University Professors, "Tenure and Teaching-Intensive Appointments," www.aaup.org/report/tenure-and-teaching-intensive-appointments.

portional expectations for service and development, and appropriately revised tenure clock. Some full-time tenure-track positions, as they become available, could be considered as split positions, even for non-married faculty whose scholarly interest might nevertheless complement each other. Such changes would allow for the flexibility necessary in today's family to better accommodate the needs of child- and eldercare, whether it be done by women *or* men. In fact, many partnered male scholars would presumably welcome the chance to shoulder more caretaking responsibilities, even as many women move (albeit gradually) into positions of greater power in the workplace more generally. This would represent a major step toward gender justice as well as support the well-being of families.

Off the tenure track, as well, universities can implement changes that would go a long way towards redressing the systemic injustices elaborated above. First and foremost, proportional pay for work done would represent a dramatic improvement for contingent faculty, many of whom currently teach large lower-division classes and thus carry an enormous teaching load for far lower pay. If, as James Keenan has pointed out, adjunct faculty represent the new "working poor," there is no substitute for ensuring that they are paid a fair wage for their work.[44] Further, the creation of preferred hiring pools for faculty who perform well, with some reasonable assurance of contract renewal if programmatic need persists, would allow contingent faculty to better plan for their own concrete needs as well as to confer an increased degree of respect for their institutional contributions. Multi-year contracts also reduce the insecurity that accompanies year-to-year, or even semester-to-semester, employment.

Still, higher pay and benefits, and even increased stability of employment, represent only a part of the strategy that colleges and universities must undertake. As Keenan rightly points out, "Tenure-track and tenured faculty as well as departmental chairs simply take for granted the secondary status of adjunct faculty."[45] This disdain manifests itself in countless ways, ranging from lack of office space or mailboxes, to exclusion from departmental meetings, to a lack of voice and vote in matters of university governance. Such disregard is perhaps even more troubling insofar as it mirrors the broader social devaluation of women's work; while certainly not all adjunct teachers are female, the feminization of this sector of academia no doubt contributes to the tendency to take their work for granted by those holding unrecognized gendered expectations.

---

[44] Keenan, *University Ethics*, 49, citing Gary Rhoades, "Adjunct Faculty are the New Working Poor," *CNN*, September 25, 2013, www.cnn.com/2013/09/24/opinion/rhoades-adjunct-faculty/index.html.
[45] Keenan, *University Ethics*, 47.

In the face of such personal and institutional challenges, tenure-stream faculty and administrators alike must therefore be invited to stand in solidarity with their adjunct colleagues. This means supporting structural changes that benefit contingent faculty, such as fair wages and benefits. It also means heeding Keenan's call to recognize that adjunct faculty are not "outsiders" or "extras," but rather are full contributors to the educational and institutional work of higher education. Often relatively minor changes—office space, name plates on doors, or even academic titles, for instance—can communicate this higher level of respect for contingent faculty. Fundamentally, tenure-stream faculty and administrators themselves must be summoned to realize the genuine ways in which contingent faculty are essential to the basic mission and work of the institution.

CONCLUSION

In an era of nearly ubiquitous economic belt-tightening, the crisis of contingency in our academic institutions is relatively unsurprising. Yet, as moral theologians, it is incumbent upon us to recognize the ways in which such belt-tightening functions to minimize the power and voice of those who may *already* be socially disempowered, in this case, disproportionately women. Further, part of our task as educators is to uncover the ways in which academic systems, structures, and expectations may unintentionally deprive our institutions of important moral perspectives, perspectives that broaden, deepen, and diversify our collective conversations, thereby contributing to a superior articulation of truth claims. In the case of contingent faculty, those perspectives often reflect relational realities that need to be acknowledged, in part because our institutions themselves can benefit from their incorporation.

It goes without saying that the changes articulated above are imperfect and incomplete. They far from guarantee that contingent faculty will be able adequately to exercise their voices within institutional settings, let alone ensuring their material well-being. Yet these changes represent a much-needed start. Most of the proposals suggested above require a commitment to creative solutions on the part of university decision makers, including the prioritization of familial relationships in new ways. As the AAUP has affirmed, "Transforming the academic workplace into one that supports family life requires substantial changes in policy and, more significantly, changes in academic culture."[46] Such changes are not beyond us; rather, the proposals above serve in part as an invitation to a new way of encountering each other and to a renewed recognition that we are stronger, both

---

[46] AAUP, "Statement of Principles on Family Responsibility and Academic Work."

institutionally and personally, when we stand together to promote our common well-being. University communities have a duty to discern the ways that our institutional systems and personal assumptions ineluctably draw upon and perpetuate gender inequity, thereby impoverishing our academic communities themselves. As moral theologians who care about the dignity, value, and rights of all persons and as educators who privilege the search for truth, it is time for us to accept the invitation.

The Spiritual Crisis of Contingent Faculty

Claire Bischoff

MANY, IF NOT MOST, OF US IN ACADEMICS are familiar with imposter syndrome, that persistent fear of being exposed as a fraud. We teach our classes, write academic papers, and conduct research waiting for the other shoe to drop, so to speak. We open our e-mail expecting a note from our dean confirming that we are not smart enough to teach the classes assigned to us or withdrawing an internal grant due to a lack of relevant skills and experience.

For me as a contingent faculty member, the ante of imposter syndrome gets raised to angst-inducing heights. I am not simply anticipating the dropping of the other shoe. I am stumbling around in a forest, dreading the moment I inadvertently walk into a trip wire that will release a guillotine blade of unemployment on my neck. Yes, this metaphor is a touch dramatic, but think about what contingent means. If you look it up, you will find that contingent means "subject to chance" and "occurring or existing only if (certain other circumstances) are the case."[1] According to this definition, as a contingent faculty member, I am in my position by happenstance. Further, if I find myself in a job only because certain circumstances are the case, it follows that new circumstances could arise at any point that would nullify my employment, circumstances over which I have little to no control. We who are subject to chance are apprenticed into constant vigilance, scanning our horizons for those certain circumstances that will lead to our redundancy.

So why disseminate my reflection here, if the potential cost of doing so could be losing a job I love? Because, while I am a contingent faculty member and thus vulnerable at my university, I am not as vulnerable in a broader sense as many other contingent faculty are. It is crucial to name that my spouse has a full-time job with benefits, so, if this article trips a wire, we still will be able to pay our mortgage and have access to health care for our children and ourselves. I have a little more freedom to speak and, as Catholic social teaching reminds me,

---

[1] "Contingent," www.google.com/search?q=contingent&oq=contingent&aqs=chrome. 69i57j0l5.1190j1j8&sourceid=chrome&ie=UTF-8.

with freedom comes responsibility.² So I write this, drawing on my experience of being a contingent faculty member at two institutions over the past six years, because I know that for many contingent faculty writing honestly about their experiences is too risky a thing to do.

My thesis is that the crisis of contingent faculty in the United States constitutes a spiritual crisis, for many contingent faculty members as individuals and also for our institutions as communities of learning. This claim is based on Roman Catholic religious sister, teacher, and scholar Thea Bowman's definition of spirituality as "at once God-awareness, self-awareness, and other-awareness."³ In my experience, being employed as a contingent faculty member has interfered with my self-awareness, other-awareness, and even God-awareness. Further, my reflections lead me to sincere concern about the ability of our academic communities to meet the needs of our students when non-tenure-track positions of all types now account for over 70 percent of instructional staff appointments in higher education in the United States.⁴ My hope in honestly illustrating how my self-, other-, and God-awareness has been challenged by my contingent employment status is that others will hear echoes of their own experiences, echoes whose reverberations will lead to action in service of addressing this spiritual crisis in whatever positions we find ourselves, in whatever ways we can.

SELF-AWARENESS

The story of the circuitous route I took to making this spiritually-grounded argument is illustrative of how being a contingent faculty member has been a roadblock to my self-awareness. Early in spring semester 2018, the chair of my department asked me if I would consider being on a panel about the crisis of contingent faculty at the annual meeting of the College Theology Society, which was to be held on our campus at the beginning of summer.⁵ The organizers of the

---

² Th reciprocal relationship between human rights (freedoms) and responsibilities is the third theme of Catholic social teaching identified by the U.S. Catholic bishops; see United States Conference of Catholic Bishops, "Seven Th mes of Catholic Social Teaching," www.usccb.org/beliefs-and-teachings/what-we-believe/catholic-social-teaching/seven-themes-of-catholic-social-teaching.cfm.
³ Th a Bowman, "Spirituality," in *Modern Spiritual Masters: Writings on Contemplation and Compassion*, ed. Robert Ellsberg (Maryknoll: Orbis Books, 2011), 133.
⁴ American Association of University Professors, "Background Facts on Contingent Faculty," www.aaup.org/issues/contingency/background-facts.
⁵ Ths journal article is adapted from my talk at this plenary panel session. I would like to thank the leadership of the College Th ology Society for giving time in the meeting program for this important topic to be discussed. Th nks also to Gerald Beyer for organizing the panel, Jason King for moderating it, and Steve Werner for sharing stories of his experience as a contingent faculty member.

panel were hoping to find someone local who had experience as a contingent faculty member; it also did not hurt that I would add some gender diversity to the all-male group of speakers already on the docket for the panel. Being keenly aware of my contingent status, I felt I needed an amazingly good reason to say no to a request from my department chair. Lacking such a reason, I said yes and promptly decided I did not have to worry about what I would say until at least the beginning of May.

As the weather finally turned warmer and the fog of the semester started to clear, I began to think in earnest about my take on the crisis of contingent faculty. Falling back on my doctoral training, I delved into research. I compiled a list of relevant and reputable articles, and even started reading a few of them, only to find myself getting apprehensive about what I could possibly add to this conversation when so many insightful analyses already had been written. I knew that I could not become an expert, in the four weeks or so I had given myself to write my remarks for the panel, in social ethics or university policy. What is a contingent faculty member to do in order to present herself as a serious scholar?

Within this question lies the seed of my lack of self-awareness, a lack stimulated by my strong consciousness of my employment status. I was approaching this task as I thought I *should* approach it, as I imagined a *true* academic would approach it. Despite the fact that academics work in a plethora of ways, there is a dominant narrative about quality scholarship that encourages us to write objective pieces grounded in research, be it in library research or quantitative and qualitative studies. As a contingent faculty member, my first instinct is to blend in, to perform this dominant narrative, even if it is not a narrative that works particularly well for me. To do otherwise feels extremely risky. I do not want to bring any undue attention to myself and possibly find myself fired because I'm not good enough, or smart enough, and doggone it, no one likes me.[6]

Thank goodness at this point in my preparations I was reminded of Sr. Thea's definition of spirituality in an undergraduate paper I was grading. The miasma surrounding my self-awareness cleared. In my concern about appearing professional, I had forgotten my actual professional identities—as a practical theologian and religious educator, as a teacher of spirituality, as a writer about theology and parenting, and as a contingent faculty member.[7] My theological method involves

---

[6] Th se who watched *Saturday Night Live* in the 1990s will recognize this phrasing, in the negative, of the catch phrase of Al Franken's character Stuart Smalley, host of the mock self-help show "Daily Affirmations with Stuart Smalley."

[7] I am all too aware that I have left off of this list of professional identities my identity as the primary caregiver for three young children, and that leaving it off of this list

looking at the minute and mundane details of everyday life and connecting these details to broader theological concepts. The only authentic way for me to contribute to the panel, as frightening and counter-academic-cultural as it seemed, was to reflect on my experience, to put these necessarily personal and emotional reflections in conversation with what I know about spirituality, and to see what emerged. The results of this process are what you are reading here.

As it was for me in the process of preparing this piece, being a contingent faculty member can be a major stumbling block to self-awareness. It may be hard for those of us who are subject to chance to do the work we are called to do. Without a system that is responsible to us, without institutions that support us in our teaching and our scholarship, our freedom to be who we are is constrained in meaningful ways. We put so much intellectual and emotional energy into staying employed that we may not have much left in the tank for attending to our authentic selves and boldly teaching, researching, and writing out of our particular gifts. Many contingent faculty manage to do so anyway, but the costs of doing so without institutional support and without the safety net of tenure are high.

There is another aspect of being a contingent faculty member that blocks self-awareness, and that is the internalizing of the common narratives that get told about us. Again, let me use a personal story to illustrate. In spring 2018, I was invited to be the speaker at Thinking Theologically, a once-a-semester event put on by the master of arts in theology program at my university, where faculty present their research to colleagues and graduate students. Rather than read my recently published essay on parenting and spirituality, which would have followed the pattern of how this event normally goes, I decided to take on the challenge of writing a draft of the next piece on parenting as spiritual practice that had been percolating within me.[8] It was a precarious choice, but the evening went well. My colleagues, in person and over e-mail, gave rave reviews about my presentation, reviews that, at first, I thought I had earned.

Then, a few days later, a new thought crept into my head: "Were they impressed just because they are used to seeing me only as a teacher and not a scholar? Was their excitement about my work

---

concedes to another dominant narrative in academics, which tells caregivers that our identities as caregivers do not matter to our professional identities as scholars and teachers. I see my personal experience as a mother and contingent faculty member represented well in Karen Peterson-Iyer's essay in this volume, entitled "Contingency, Gender, and the Academic Table."

[8] Claire Bischoff, "Awake My Soul: Mothering Myself Toward Recovery," in *Parenting as Spiritual Practice and Source for Theology: Mothering Matters*, ed. Claire Bischoff, Annie Hardison-Moody, and Elizabeth Gandolfo (New York: Palgrave Macmillan, 2017).

heightened because they did not expect that I could do this sort of work at all?" As these demeaning questions swirled in my head, I realized that I had fully imbibed some of the common narrative myths about contingent faculty: we are working as contingent employees because we could not get jobs anywhere else; we might be decent teachers, but we do not cut it as scholars; we are second-class academics; we are less than. A two-tiered academic hierarchy of contingent and non-contingent faculty will only continue to degrade the self-awareness that contingent faculty have. When we are treated long enough as less than, we may come to believe this as the truth and may struggle to see ourselves as made wonderfully in the image of God, just as we are.[9]

OTHER-AWARENESS

In addition to eroding self-awareness, being a contingent faculty member also affects our awareness of others but in the opposite direction. Instead of not being aware of others, my contention is that operating from second-class positions as contingent faculty makes us hyper-aware of our students and faculty colleagues. This hyper-awareness makes it challenging to enter into the sort of authentic relationships with our students and colleagues that best meet the needs of our students and our schools.

Awareness of Students

Let me start with an example about relating to students. Last fall I had a small vocational crisis. One section of introductory theology, for reasons I could not discern clearly at the time, made me doubt myself as a teacher. Toward the end of the semester, there were days when I had to force myself to go to class, so strong was my anxiety about standing up in front of these women and teaching theology.

Over January, as I prepared the syllabus for the next iteration of this course, I was able to untangle some of the threads of my disquiet from the past semester. I had become debilitatingly focused on teaching toward the experience of my students. Of course, there are important cultural factors that contribute to my over-attention to student

---

[9] I am basing this theological anthropological claim on the first principle of Catholic social teaching: the dignity of the human person. In turn, this claim about the inherent dignity of each person is based on the biblical narrative in Genesis 1:26-31 of God creating all human beings in God's image. See United States Conference of Catholic Bishops, "Seven Th mes of Catholic Social Teaching," www.usccb.org/beliefs-and-teachings/what-we-believe/catholic-social-teaching/seven-themes-of-catholic-social-teaching.cfm. For an insightful treatment of the complicated history of this theological anthropological belief from a feminist lens, see Michelle Gonzalez, *Created in God's Image: An Introduction to Feminist Th ological Anthropology* (Maryknoll: Orbis Books, 2007).

experience—like the fact that millennials have the reputation for prioritizing experience over all else.[10] Further, our students are dealing with anxiety, depression, eating disorders, and other mental health challenges at higher rates than ever before.[11] As a teacher of spirituality, I see it as part and parcel of my work to provide a class experience that resonates with the spiritual content of the course, as well as to introduce students to specific spiritual practices that may help meet their needs as spiritual human beings.

That being said, a major factor in my hyper-attention to student experience is that no matter how brilliant a paper I gave at the Thinking Theologically night, it is the students' end-of-semester evaluations of my teaching that keep me in a job. My colleagues think of me as a good teacher, but most have never seen me teach. Because of this I have to assume that they take my students' word for it that I am doing passably well in the classroom.

When I emphasize student experience to such a large extent, I treat students as a group of consumers rather than as a learning community made up of people who all have wisdom to share. I put on a show based on what I think they want to see in the classroom rather than teaching from an authentic place grounded in who I am as an educator. I cheat them out of the chance to be challenged and transformed because I am too worried about offering a palatable experience that will rank well on the end-of-semester bubble sheet.

Many of the best educators I know are employed in contingent positions and do a masterful job of attending to the real needs and desires of their students. The problem is that contingent faculty are hampered by being employed in a system that is not set up to support us taking the sorts of risks in the classroom that are necessary for transformative learning. Many of us rise to the occasion and bravely do the sort of teaching that truly balances awareness of our students, awareness of our own teaching strengths, and awareness of the truths of our curricula. Often, we do this at our own peril and without sufficient financial and institutional support.

Awareness of Faculty Colleagues

Similar to the pull to be hyper-aware of our students' experiences, we become hyper-aware of our faculty colleagues' predilections, particularly of those who are in positions of power over us. While we may

---

[10] See, for instance, this Harris poll conducted on behalf of Eventbrite: "Millennials: Fueling the Experience Economy," eventbrite-s3.s3.amazonaws.com/marketing/Millennials_Research/Gen_PR_Final.pdf.

[11] See, for instance, Katie Reilly, "Record Numbers of College Students Are Seeking Treatment for Depression and Anxiety — But Schools Can't Keep Up," *Time*, March 19, 2018, time.com/5190291/anxiety-depression-college-university-students/.

enjoy these colleagues on a personal level, we end up relating to their power positions rather than to their individual humanity as a means of job protection. Let me offer one brief exemplification.

A few years ago, I was invited by the director of a program in which I taught to be part of a committee that would be reevaluating a portion of our curriculum. Again, when someone in a position of power asks you to take part in something, you need an amazingly good reason to say no. Again, I did not have one, so I said yes, even though this was an additional job responsibility for which I would receive no extra remuneration. I was joined on this committee by another contingent faculty member and someone who was pre-tenure. The three of us met, and the theme of our meeting was a sense of powerlessness. The recommendation we wanted to offer ran counter to what we knew the director of the program thought was best. None of us had any reason to mistrust this individual based on our personal dealings, and yet all of us mistrusted this person based on the position of power he held. None of us were sure if making an against-the-grain recommendation, one we were convinced was in service of bettering the program, would be the action that tripped the wire of unemployment.

To refer back to a statistic I cited earlier, non-tenure-track positions of all types now account for over 70 percent of all instructional staff appointments in higher education in the United States.[12] We are in real spiritual trouble at our schools if this high of a proportion of faculty do not have the institutional support necessary to speak their truths and to engage in dialogue about the betterment of our institutions with our tenured and tenure-track colleagues.

Our inability as contingent faculty to be aware of our colleagues as children of God, wonderful just as they are, is not only about our own fear. Unfortunately, many of us have also experienced micro-aggressions from our faculty colleagues that serve to remind us, whether intentionally or not, that we are second-class citizens in the academy. I personally have experienced and also witnessed other contingent faculty colleagues being talked over, having our ideas not taken seriously, and having our experiences re-interpreted for us by tenured faculty members. While these "small slights" may seem trivial and may not even be noticed by the contingent faculty member at the time, research has indicated that these sorts of micro-aggressions "have a powerful impact on the psychological well-being of marginalized groups."[13] I have doubts about the possibility of contingent faculty members

---

[12] American Association of University Professors, "Background Facts on Contingent Faculty," www.aaup.org/issues/contingency/background-facts.

[13] Derald Wing Sue, "Microaggressions: More than Just Race," www.psychologytoday.com/us/blog/microaggressions-in-everyday-life/201011/microaggressions-more-just-race.

achieving any strong measure of authentic other-awareness with our tenured colleagues as long as this two-tiered hierarchy exists.

GOD-AWARENESS

You will recall that my thesis—that the crisis with contingent faculty in the U.S. is a spiritual crisis—is based on Sr. Thea Bowman's definition of spirituality as self-awareness, other-awareness, and God-awareness. You also may have noticed a theme throughout this reflection: fear. Contingent faculty live with almost constant fear: fear of being ourselves, fear of disappointing our students, fear of upsetting our colleagues. It is this fear that most disrupts our God-awareness.

First, fear limits our ability to experience the immanence of God. When we cannot focus on being our authentic selves and when we are too hyper-focused on the experiences of our students and the penchants of our colleagues, there is little to no room for the intimate presence of God in our lives. We still may feel God transcendently, still may trust that God is out there being God, but we have lost the place for God in ourselves and the capacity to see God in others. The effect is a reduction rather than an expansion in our knowledge of and faith in God.

Second, if we are made in the image of God and conformed to the likeness of Christ, as the Christian biblical witness and centuries of tradition proclaim, then we are molded in radical creativity and holy boldness. Living in fear damages our *imago Dei*, dims the light of our Spirits, and inhibits us from walking the prophetic path to which the Gospels call us. In our fear, in the no person's land of contingency, we do not have the institutional support to call out old systems of power or to make things new. In resignation, we may live the way of the status quo, which is not the way of the kingdom of God.

It is a relatively common colloquialism that it is fear, and not hate or indifference, which is the opposite of love.[14] I believe in a God who is Love. When I live in fear, I do not live out of and into this Love. What is God's love like? God's love is known by God's actions. God's love is not a warm and fuzzy feeling on a Hallmark card, but the determination to make things right. What would it mean for those of us in the academy to live beyond our fears and out of God's love? What

---

[14] Ths idea has been promoted through the writings of contemporary and popular spiritual teachers such as Eckhart Tolle and Marianne Williamson. See Eckhart Tolle, *A New Earth: Awakening to Your Life's Purpose* (New York: Penguin Books, 2005) and Marianne Williamson, *A Return to Love: Reflections on the Principles of A Course in Miracles* (New York: HarperOne, 1996).

would it look like to trust, along with Dorothy Day, that "love and ever more love is the only solution to every problem that comes up"?[15]

In case I sound naïve and overly sentimental in calling for those of us in the academy to live out of God's love, let me first mention St. Thérèse of Lisieux, who is often thought naïve and overly sentimental for her proposal of "the little way" of surrendering to and living out of the love of God in whatever situation we find ourselves.[16] Thérèse lived with the "complete conviction that it is not so much what we do that counts in God's eyes but rather the love with which we do it."[17] Perhaps because of her nickname, "the Little Flower," and the emphasis on the concept of spiritual childhood in her spiritual autobiography,[18] Thérèse is often pictured as "a very naïve, innocent, and over-pious little girl. Her spirituality is then pictured the same way. Her little way is conceived of as the quiet, innocent, anonymous martyrdom of obscurity, that is, a spirituality of doing simple, menial-type work for God without expecting to be noticed."[19] Yet there is nothing simple or sentimental about surrendering the self to the love of God and trusting the will of God with profound confidence, two ways of being that are at the heart of Thérèse's "little way."[20] As one Thérèse scholar puts it, "Her 'little way' becomes the way of loving abandonment into God's waiting arms. Such a way demands sacrifice, suffering, true and profound charity."[21] To surrender to the love of God, especially in the academy, is not a path for the faint of heart.

Lest this path of surrendering to love seems a calling only for the saintliest among us, let me offer one final story, about a recent time that I was a recipient of this radical living out of love. This past year financial trouble at my institution necessitated some draconian

---

[15] Dorothy Day, "On Pilgrimage," in *Modern Spiritual Masters: Writings on Contemplation and Compassion*, ed. Robert Ellsberg (Maryknoll: Orbis Books, 2011), 178.

[16] In her autobiography, Th rèse writes, "How different are the ways through which the Lord leads souls!" She believed that God respected the myriad of ways in which people followed the way of Jesus in their particular life situations. See Th rèse of Lisieux, *Story of a Soul: Th Autobiography of St. Th rèse of Lisieux*, trans. John Clarke, O.C.D. (Washington, D.C.: ICS Publications, 1996), 207.

[17] Louis Dupré and James A. Wiseman, O.S.B., "Th rèse of Lisieux," in *Light from Light: An Anthology of Christian Mysticism*, 2nd ed., ed. Louis Dupré and James A. Wiseman, O.S.B. (New York: Paulist Press, 2001), 413.

[18] For an accessible introduction to the idea of spiritual childhood in Th rèse's writing, see John F. Russell, "Th rèse of Lisieux and Spiritual Childhood," *Spiritual Life* 40 (1994): 7-12.

[19] Ronald Rolheiser, "Key Elements in Th rèse's Spirituality," ronrolheiser.com/me/uploads/2014/02/key_elements.pdf.

[20] An important text that speaks to the surrendering to love at the heart of Th rèse's spirituality is her "Act of Oblation to Merciful Love," *Story of a Soul*, 276-277.

[21] Th mas H. Morris, "Th rèse's Story of a Soul: Wisdom for Today," *Spiritual Life* 33 (1987): 89-96.

measures to be taken in order to move toward a balanced budget. Every department across the university was given the mandate to reduce, and, in our small department of eight faculty, those in leadership in the department were asked to reduce us by the equivalent of one full-time position. There would have been an easy way to make this cut; those in leadership could have opted not to renew my contract for the following year. As the most recent hire in the department, they could have let me go. Last in, first out. That is a status quo narrative with which we are all familiar and even relatively comfortable.

Yet, moved by the Spirit, those in leadership got creative. They asked every person in the department to give something: some of us gave up our full-time status, some of us gave up course releases, some of us raised the maximum number of students in our classes so that we were, in effect, teaching an overload. By everyone giving something, we all got to keep our jobs (if not our full pay checks) for the coming year. I went from a full-time to a two-thirds-time employee so that I could keep a job. There is nothing particularly admirable about that. What was so moving to me was that my tenured colleagues entered into solidarity with me and the other contingent faculty in our department by giving up things they would not have had to give up.

Based on the standards of the world in which we live, this may not seem like much. Our theology department has not made an appreciable dent in the crisis of contingent faculty. We may only have bought some of us one more year of employment at our institution, and, yet, by the standards of Catholic spirituality, this has made all of the difference in the world. Honestly, the acts of love by my colleagues are instrumental in me being able to write the truth about my experiences as a contingent faculty. These acts of love have made a department of individuals into a community in which we have all made sacrifices for the good of each other and, hopefully, for the good of our students and our university.

We all exercise our freedom within systems of meaningful constraints.[22] There are serious cultural, institutional, financial, personal,

---

[22] Here I adapt ethnographer Wynne Maggi's understanding of freedom, which she developed through her work with the Kalasha people, a small religious-ethnic minority living in Pakistan surrounded by their more conservative Muslim neighbors. At the heart of Maggi's work is the claim of the Kalasha people that what makes them different from their Muslim neighbors is that Kalasha women are free. By investigating this claim and interrogating her own Western feminist bias about the meaning of women's freedom, Maggi comes to an understanding of freedom that helpfully keeps in view both individual agency and systems of meaningful cultural constraints. In relation to the crisis of contingent faculty in the U.S., I find this understanding of freedom to be refreshing, as it reminds those of us in positions of contingency, as well as those in positions of relative power, that we do have a modicum of agency, while also being realistic about meaningful constraints on this agency. See Wynne Maggi, *Our*

and interpersonal factors that work against our freedom to respond to the spiritual crisis that faces us in higher education as a result of our dependence on contingent faculty. Yet ... the *Journal of Moral Theology* decided to do this issue, and you are choosing to read it. Some people in my department did something hard so that we truly were in solidarity with each other. My challenge to all of us is to think seriously and strategically about and then to act boldly and with love in response to this spiritual crisis. Particularly for those of you in positions of relative power, I invite you to think about what solidarity looks like in your context. We all face systems of constraint that limit our freedom and make us fearful, but we are also all children of God, made lovely as we are, who can find creative, redemptive, and spirit-filled ways to live with a love that will invite greater awareness of self, others, and God.

Women Are Free: Gender and Ethnicity in the Hindukush (Ann Arbor: University of Michigan Press, 2001), 40-43.

Departmental Chair as Faculty Advocate and Middle Manager

Elizabeth Hinson-Hasty

WHEN I WAS ASKED TO REFLECT as a department chair on my work with contingent faculty, I first began writing an essay that clearly passed judgment upon consumer-driven, market-oriented models for making decisions about university programs and the unjust treatment of adjuncts. I think it is important to begin by explaining why my comments will be more measured here. I soon realized in the process of conducting my research and reflecting on my experiences as an academic leader that my observations would be inauthentic if I did not place myself squarely in the middle of the conversation. As an academic leader, tenured full professor, and senior member of the department, I am dependent upon the institution that I serve for my own livelihood and benefit from hiring practices, pay scales, sabbatical policies, and teaching schedules biased in favor of fulltime faculty. The fact that I am a Reformed scholar who researches historical and contemporary issues related to economic ethics adds another layer of complexity to the conversation. Concepts of the preferential option for people in poverty and just solidarity, two basic principles of Catholic social teaching, are foundational to my scholarly work. These concepts serve as more than a theoretical lens; they are social commitments that demand action. However, clear pathways for action within the university are not always obvious due to a variety of factors, including the dependence of tenured professors upon the institutions they serve to secure their own livelihoods, lack of access for chairs to decision-making groups that determine salaries, and the broader disinvestment in higher education in the U.S.

My effort in these pages is to reflect authentically and honestly out of my own experience about the cognitive dissonance and moral incoherence one encounters when navigating two worlds—the world of tenured faculty and the world of contingency. I argue that chairs and other tenured faculty members must examine their own privilege, leverage that privilege to create more just employment policies for faculty and staff within the university as a whole, and begin to identify the interests of faculty with the larger common good of the university.

I consider concrete ways chairs can alleviate the circumstances of contingent faculty as well as wrestle with the role of a chair as both faculty advocate and middle manager. Department chairs should engage in reflective practice and advocacy for a university community that holds the values of fairness, reciprocity, collaboration, interdependence, accountability to a larger community, sustainability, and the inclusion of diverse peoples and experiences at the center of its mission.

CONSIDERING THE BROADER CONTEXT FOR DISCUSSIONS ABOUT FACULTY PAY

There are a number of factors that inform the broader context for discussions about faculty (fulltime and part-time) pay that must at least be named even if their implications cannot be fully explored in this essay. Worldwide, there is a trend toward disinvestment in higher education that reflects neoliberal economic policies that, among other things, question the responsibility of the state as the provider of social needs, favor the privatization of public good and services, and emphasize free markets as the most rational and democratic system of choice. Bruce Johnstone, former Chancellor of the State University of New York, observes that in the twenty first century "Governments are ... besieged with other pressing public needs, many of which seem more politically compelling than the claims of higher education, and which, together with higher education, greatly exceed, in almost all countries, the available scarce public revenues."[1] The result is what Johnstone calls "extreme austerity" within universities. Institutions are held under constant scrutiny to be accountable and responsive to students and their parents, the government, and the academic community. Individuals and families increasingly bear a heavier share of the cost of a university education. There is a popular and pervasive narrative that liberal arts education is impractical and outdated and that academic institutions should offer more majors and programs that appeal to employers, due to both cost and limited resources.

At the same time, colleges and universities recruit students within the highly competitive environment where programs and services must match what is available at other institutions. Declining state support and extremely competitive markets for students leads to concerns about sustainability. Indeed, there are significant differences in the financial stability and sustainability of well-endowed institution and tuition dependent ones. More than 40 percent of all Catholic institutions of higher education in the U.S. have endowments of less than $25 million. Inside Higher Ed and Gallup polled the Chief Financial Officers of 438 colleges and universities in 2014 and found that only 13 percent

---

[1] D. Bruce Johnstone, "The Economics and Politics of Cost-Sharing in Higher Education: Comparative Perspective," *Economics of Education Review* 23 (2004): 403.

felt confident in their financial model over the next 10 years.[2] The survey was prompted at least in part after the announcement of the closure of Sweet Briar College, which later reopened because of alumnae pressure.

Much more could be said here. My intent is to suggest that these factors point to why administrators and boards look to economics and finance to reshape their business models. Business models and business interests are radically reshaping higher education, including the professoriate, program development, and deployment and employment practices.[3] Many scholars comment on the changing nature of and business models for U.S. higher education that reflect broader trends in society which open every domain in life to evaluation by market-based logic, the measurement of success in terms of growth, and a focus on individual prosperity.[4] Ethicist James Keenan writes about commodification as a mindset:

> The university aims not at its mission, that is, the education of its citizenry to promote the common good, but at its own financial survival. Subsequently the geography of the campus shifts with more staff and more managers providing students a wider array of services, from health care, extracurricular activities, police safety, varied dining service, sports facilities, housing opportunities, career and personal counseling, and technological support, among other services.[5]

I have argued elsewhere that economism as an "ism" prioritizes economics as the discipline with the best knowledge to lead to institutional flourishing and emphasizes the monetization of all things at the expense of nonmonetary values such as community, fairness, justice, and love.[6] From an ethical perspective, this leads to questions about whether or not economics and business models alone can lead to just employment practices and build authentic communities of learning as

---

[2] Mark Toner, "The Highly Endangered Higher Education Business Model (And How to Fix It)," American Council on Education, www.acenet.edu/the-presidency/columns-and-features/Pages/The-Highly-Endangered-Higher-Education-Business-Model.aspx.

[3] See The Brookings Institution, "Disruptive Innovations in Higher Education," www.brookings.edu/series/disruptive-innovations-in-higher-education/.

[4] One of my favorite texts to use in class is Michael Sandel's, *What Money Can't Buy: The Moral Limits of Markets* (New York: Farrar, Strauss, and Giroux, 2012).

[5] James Keenan, *University Ethics: How Colleges Can Build and Benefit from a Culture of Ethics* (Lanham: Rowman and Littlefield, 2015), 174.

[6] See Elizabeth Hinson-Hasty, *The Problem of Wealth: A Christian Response to a Culture of Affluence* (Maryknoll: Orbis Books, 2017), 51.

well as how chairs and other academic leaders can envision alternatives and affect the current consumer-driven trajectory of higher education.

COURSE CANCELLATION AND THE CHALLENGES CHAIRS FACE

Let me offer a concrete example of the difficult space in which chairs often find themselves within a tuition dependent university when working with contingent faculty. Last fall, I was faced with an ethical decision just before the beginning of the semester when the dean's office asked me to cancel a class due to low enrollment. The course subject to cancellation was to be taught by one of my fulltime tenured colleagues. Cancelling classes occurs infrequently in our department because Bellarmine, like most Catholic universities, requires two theology classes within the General Education program, so I asked for recommendations about making up the three hours of teaching load for the colleague who teaches fulltime. One of two recommendations given to me was to cancel an adjunct faculty member's contract and to put my fulltime tenured colleague on the schedule in his place. The second option was for my fulltime colleague to make up the three hours of her teaching load within two years.

I felt conflicted as department chair by these two options because I was well aware that my part-time colleague depends upon the income. Removing him from the course was a question of justice and equity for me. Ordinarily, he teaches five or six classes a semester at three or four different institutions. The timing of the cancellation meant that it was too late to schedule a class at another institution. Several questions about basic needs entered my mind due to my awareness that 31 percent of contingent faculty live near or below the poverty line.[7] About 25 percent of adjunct faculty receive public assistance.[8] If I enact the university policy reflected in option one, will he have enough money to pay his mortgage or to buy groceries and gas for his car? How would my decision affect his ability to be able to pay for things like health care premiums or prescriptions? At the same time, I work alongside my fulltime tenured colleague and felt a loyalty to her. I am aware of the significant amount of time and energy she devotes to students and on behalf of our department. My conversation with the associate dean about these issues ended with the abrupt realization that "it's the industry standard."

---

[7] Caroline Frederickson, "There is No Excuse for How Universities Treat Adjuncts," *The Atlantic*, September 15, 2015, www.theatlantic.com/business/archive/2015/09/higher-education-college-adjunct-professor-salary/404461/.

[8] Kevin Birmingham, "'The Great Shame of Our Profession': How the Humanities Survive on Exploitation," *The Chronicle of Higher Education*, February 12, 2017, www.chronicle.com/article/The-Great-Shame-of-Our/239148.

You may have been aware of these issues for some time if you have served as a chair, in another position of academic leadership, or as an adjunct faculty member, but my experience of fourteen years of teaching at a university compares more to that of Keenan. He writes,

> The gulf between tenured faculty and adjunct faculty has few secured ways of passage connecting us. I know little about the terms of their employment. Like other tenured faculty I have consciously and unconsciously, and conveniently, worn blinders about their work and their context.[9]

Indeed, I found out through some minimal research that replacing adjunct faculty with fulltime faculty in the course cancellation process is a common practice, "the industry standard"; this is one way that tuition dependent universities deal with fluctuating student enrollment. Most often, little or no attention is given to course preparation that a part-time faculty member has already invested in the class. Some schools deal with this issue by offering minimal compensation for a course cancelled close to the beginning of the semester.[10]

Chairs confront a significant challenge here as we have little authority to challenge policies and practices related to course cancellation beyond ensuring that the university honors minimum enrollments previously established. Our duties, at least at smaller universities, do not include establishing rates of pay. The university defines the role of chair primarily as middle manager.

THE ROLE OF CHAIR AS MIDDLE MANAGER

The idea that upper administrators or colleagues would define and see my role in terms of "middle management" was far from my mind when I accepted the appointment as department chair. I approached my work with a sense of tenured professorial exceptionalism formed by memories of one parent's career as an academic all-star and my early pre-tenure participation in faculty groups centering on Parker Palmer's book *The Courage to Teach*. At first, I thought of chairs as visionaries for the department. Most professors do accept the position for intrinsic reasons because they see the position "as an opportunity

---

[9] Keenan, *University Ethics*, 39.
[10] Some institutions offer some pay to part-time faculty when course cancellation occurs with a few weeks before or just after the beginning of the semester. For example, when a course is cancelled within seven days of the start of class a part-time faculty member gets one sixteenth of his or her pay. See Colleen Flaherty, "Contracts Up Close," *Inside Higher Ed*, April 21, 2015, www.insidehighered.com/news/2015/04/21/labor-conference-panel-centers-contract-provisions-adjuncts-course-cancellation.

to help either their departments or themselves."[11] There is some of that as one creates an atmosphere that fosters collaborative work as a team, plans academic schedules, and takes charge of hiring faculty to teach particular classes. However, within the first year of my appointment, I discovered that chairs are evaluated primarily based on their efficiency, communication, and ability to implement academic policies.[12]

The expectation and demand for efficiency and long list of duties for chairs means that we have little time or energy to be visionaries and seek alternative ways to address the circumstance of contingent faculty. Walter Gmelch and Val Miskin, leading researchers in academic leadership, describe four roles of department chairs, which include faculty developer, manager, leader, and scholar; three-fourths of the job is managerial in nature.[13] Eighty-six percent of chairs limit their own scholarly activities in order to lead their departments.[14] Personally, I felt that I had to continue my scholarship in addition to fulfilling duties as chair because I am the first woman and Protestant to occupy the position at my institution.

My institution does better than most in helping chairs and program directors think about balancing their roles as both middle managers and faculty advocates, but we are primarily evaluated for our efficiency and productivity. Universities and colleges list an average of about twenty-five duties for department chairs.[15] The duties for which chairs are responsible and the demand for efficiency make it increasingly difficult to build relationships with our colleagues, attend to their individual needs as human beings, and envision innovative alternatives to the scarcity that defines the experience of most adjuncts. I was reminded of this during the week that the fall schedule was due when an adjunct faculty member who teaches for us on a regular basis stopped by my office because he needed to pick up a class. He was unable to teach the previous semester and, for the sake of my own efficiency and due to time constraints, I scheduled classes only for those who were already listed on the prepopulated schedule. When I

---

[11] Walter H. Gmelch and Val D. Miskin, *Department Chair Leadership Skills* (Madison: Atwood Publishing, 2011), 6.
[12] It is worth mentioning here that I am challenging a definition of efficiency that does not allow enough time for chairs to consider faculty/employees as human beings with encumbrances and needs. When I invited one of the deans of my college to review my paper, she made an important observation that sometimes efficiency is important when other employees need to rely on information provided by chairs, such as the timeliness of schedules, in order to do their jobs.
[13] Gmelch and Miskin, *Department Chair Leadership Skills*, 10.
[14] Gmelch and Miskin, *Department Chair Leadership Skills*, 11.
[15] This information was provided at a Workshop for Department and Division Chairs organized by the Council of Independent Colleges (2014), Baltimore, Maryland.

realized what I had done, I apologized profusely. He said, "I understand how it works. Out of sight, out of mind." His observation punctuated for me the invisibility of contingent faculty in the larger decision-making processes in the university, the precarity of their positions, and my own limitations.

Part of the conflict that I describe here in terms of my own understanding of the role of chair as middle manager versus visionary reflects the transition within universities toward the business model. Business dictionaries define middle managers as "an employee of an organization or business who manages at least one subordinate level of managers, and reports to a higher level of managers within the organization. The duties of a middle manager typically include carrying out the strategic directives of upper-level managers at the operational level, supervising subordinate managers and employees to ensure smooth functioning of the enterprise."[16] Most of the list of duties for chairs within university or departmental handbooks relates to timeliness, attention to detail, efficiency, program growth, compliance with assessment procedures, the ability to deal appropriately with conflict, and the ability to manage departmental budgets and develop business plans for new programming. In other words, the nature of the professoriate has already changed.

TENURED PROFESSORS ARE AN EXCEPTION TO THE RULE THESE DAYS

Researcher Adrianna Kezar cites the causes for the creation of new models for the professoriate in her summary of a recent study on changing models of teaching conducted by the TIAA Institute: "massification of higher education, enrollment fluctuations, dwindling resources, corporatization, technological advances, and competition from the for-profit sector."[17] Four teaching models that have emerged outside of the tenure track model include "the adjunct model, the full-time non-tenure track model, the medical/clinical model, and the for-profit/online model."[18] One of the biggest issues that Kezar highlights is that the new models are not designed with "long term institutional goals in mind."[19] An additional report written by Kezar with Elizabeth Holcomb and Daniel Maxey suggests that it highly unlikely that universities will return "to a largely tenure-track faculty model ... given

---

[16] "Middle Manager," *The Business Dictionary*, www.businessdictionary.com/definition/middle-manager.html.
[17] Adrianna Kezar, "Changing Faculty Workforce Models," *TIAA CREF Institute*, www.tiaainstitute.org/sites/default/files/presentations/2017-02/changing-faculty-workforce-models.pdf.
[18] Kezar, "Changing Faculty Workforce Models."
[19] Kezar, "Changing Faculty Workforce Models."

current economic realities; concerns with the tenure-track model's lack of flexibility; and priorities of policymakers, legislators, and academic administrators."[20]

You are likely aware that in spite of these trends the conversation on college and university campuses about faculty issues, pay, and other needs most frequently assumes that tenured or tenure-track positions are still the norm for faculty and represent the majority of faculty. The truth is that tenured professors are an exception to the rule these days, but I think that few established tenured faculty are aware of just how much the professoriate has changed.

The American Association of University Professors had found that "Since 1975, tenure and tenure-track professors have gone from roughly 45 percent of all teaching staff to less than a quarter. Meanwhile, part-time faculty are now more than 40 percent of college instructors."[21] The majority of studies that I reviewed concluded that contingent faculty, both part-time and full-time, make up more than 70 percent of those teaching in U.S. colleges and universities. Some researchers and studies even more grim estimates that tenured faculty make up only 14 percent of those teaching at U.S. universities. There is an important additional observation worth making here that distinctions must be made in our debate about fair pay between contingent faculty who depend upon teaching for their livelihood and those who have fulltime positions and teach a particular course because of their expertise. For example, this happens often in schools with professional programs such as nursing, medicine, and sometimes in theological schools where professionals offer their practical advice in clinical, preaching, etc. Moreover, it is also noteworthy that the greatest growth in contingent faculty does not occur during times of economic crisis at a university or college, but instead when the institution is financially better off.

WHY DEPARTMENT CHAIRS AND FACULTY CAN'T JUST DIG IN OUR HEELS AND CALL FOR A RETURN TO A PAST ROMANTICIZED MEMORY OF TENURE

In light of these trends and statistics, department chairs and faculty may be tempted to dig in our heels and advocate for a return to an

---

[20] Adrianna Kezar, Elizabeth Holcombe, Daniel Maxey, "Rethinking Faculty Models/Roles: An Emerging Consensus about Future Directions of the Professoriate," *TIAA Institute*, www.tiaainstitute.org/sites/default/files/presentations/2017-02/rethinking_faculty_models_roles.pdf.

[21] Jordan Weissmann, "The Ever Shrinking Role of Tenured College Professors (in 1 Chart)," *The Atlantic*, April 10, 2013, www.theatlantic.com/business/archive/2013/04/the-ever-shrinking-role-of-tenured-college-professors-in-1-chart/274849/.

earlier era in the university. Advocacy work certainly needs to done, but I want to offer some caution here for chairs and other faculty members not to call simply for a return to a past model for fulltime tenured faculty as we lament the increasingly contingent nature of the professoriate. One reason is the need to challenge tenured professorial exceptionalism.

Universities can play a significant role in social change, but they are also a microcosm of what is happening in the broader society and the trust of market-oriented logic that pervades discussions of education, health care, politics, immigration, etc. The value of work in our society is almost exclusively defined in money terms. We, as professors, are workers in the professional managerial sector. Long-term worker relationships in the U.S. have been on the decline for decades.[22] Should we be surprised that the academy reflects these broader trends? I imagine that many of us are not. We need to be aware that the nature of the professoriate is changing in similar ways as the nature of the relationship of other workers to their employers. Our task as academics is to engage the more reflective questions. We need to invite vigorous discussion of philosophical as well as systemic and structural issues in an effort to advocate for a professoriate, universities, as well as for workers in other employment sectors.

It is worth asking in this discussion of contingent faculty, fulltime and part-time, versus tenured and tenure track faculty whether or not values of fairness, justice, and inclusion have always been secured by the tenure system for faculty. The fulltime tenured model is far from an ideal form and norm for work. Let me offer a few examples. In the U.S., white women were not allowed to attend four-year colleges until the mid-nineteenth century. It took even longer for African American women to have access to the education necessary to earn bachelor's degrees. This delayed the time for women to enter the professoriate and to begin to make an imprint on higher education. Tenure for women at our nation's leading institutions only began to be awarded in the late 1940s. Helen Maud Cam was the first woman tenured at Harvard in 1948. In the 1950s, Bessie Lee Gambrill became the first woman to be tenured at Yale in a subject other than nursing; it was not until 1970 that a woman was hired as full professor at that institution.

---

[22] See Richard Wartzman, *The Rise and Fall of Good Jobs in America*; Derek Thompson, "Where Did All the Workers Go: 60 Years of Economic Change," *The Atlantic*, January 26, 2012, www.theatlantic.com/business/archive/2012/01/where-did-all-the-workers-go-60-years-of-economic-change-in-1-graph/252018/.

The Chronicle of Higher Education reported that in 2016 that 75 percent of fulltime faculty were white.[23] These facts cause me to raise questions about the most ideal and important aspects of the tenure system.

The AAUP suggests that some scholars are able to consider only contingent status because of care-giving responsibilities and other encumbrances on their lives. Responsibilities as a parent or for other family members prevents these scholars from a position that would require them to be evaluated on their teaching, service, and scholarship. Ethicist Karen Peterson-Iyer observes in her essay in this volume on "Contingency, Gender, and the Academic Table," that "as of 2008, women were ten to fifteen percent more likely to work contingently than their male academic counterparts" and "make up less than 42 percent of tenure-track faculty" and "far, far less (26 percent) of full professorships."[24]

A small group of colleagues is working on progressive policies for family leave and tenure-clock release at my university. In our meetings, younger male and female faculty have shared their own feelings of guilt for needing time off after the birth or adoption of a child or to care for other family members. These feelings are accentuated for women in their forties who fear that, if they wait to have children until after they earn tenure, they will no longer be able to do so. Many of my younger colleagues refuse to take the time off that the university currently allows because they fear being judged by a norm for tenure-track faculty that was formed years ago when dual earner couples headed few households and many professors relied upon spouses who worked at home fulltime.

I offer these observations to say that my hope is for chairs and other academic leaders to consider more broadly and deeply during this time of transition in the academy more models for faculty roles that provide for full inclusion, access in the curricular decision-making process, security, benefits, flexibility, support for research, respect, due process protections, and office space. Parker Palmer, Founder and Senior Partner Emeritus of the Center for Courage and Renewal, suggests, "The growth of any craft depends on shared practice and honest dialogue among the people who do it. We grow by private trial and error, to be sure – but our willingness to try, and fail, as individuals is severely limited when we are not supported by a community that encourages

---

[23] Ben Myers, "Where are the Minority Professors?" *The Chronicle of Higher Education*, February 14, 2016, www.chronicle.com/interactives/where-are-the-minority-professors.

[24] Karen Peterson-Iyer, "Contingency, Gender, and the Academic Table," *Journal of Moral Theology* 8, special issue no. 1 (2019): 92-114.

such risks."[25] Chairs can and should leverage our privilege to advocate for just models of the professoriate that reflect the true value of our work, will sustain a university's long-term goals, and create authentic community.

SPECIFIC WAYS CHAIRS CAN BEGIN TO LEVERAGE THEIR OWN PRIVILEGE

The greatest privilege of chairs is having a bird's eye view of the relationship of a department's work to a larger whole, and one of our most potent powers is to persuade. A common response of tenured fulltime faculty is to direct most of our attention and energy toward the distribution of resources at the university and reducing administrative costs. Keenan points out, "There were about 250,000 administrators and professional staff members in 1975, about half the number of professors, by 2005 there were over 750,000, easily outnumbering tenure-track professors."[26] Addressing this is a key aspect of the work of academic leadership, but it is not the only one. I will offer here several additional suggestions for specific things that chairs can and should do to leverage their privilege and work toward greater economic justice within the university as a whole.

Christian theologians and ethicists need to develop the vocabulary to speak across lines of disciplinary difference within the university.

Theologians in the middle ages claimed theology as "queen of the sciences," but theologians and ethicists teaching at liberal arts colleges and universities in the twenty first century are now far more marginal in the academy. In 2012, the Society of Christian Ethics instigated a committee on the Future of Christian Ethics as a field to study trends in Ph.D. production, job placement, and job creation at seminaries, divinity schools and universities. The report showed that between 2001 and 2012 job postings listed in Openings of the American Academy of Religion showed that "free-standing seminaries and even Divinity schools are shifting their lines away from ethics and toward other specializations more directed towards successful church management."[27] Of the jobs posted, "50 percent of jobs on average are being offered by Catholic institutions, followed by secular and Protestant institutions, in the 10-30 percent range from year to year."[28] Many colleges and universities debate the cost-effectiveness of offering theology and

---

[25] Parker Palmer, *The Courage to Teach* (San Francisco: Jossey Bass, 2017), 144.
[26] Keenan, *University Ethics*, 67.
[27] The Society of Christian Ethics, "2020 Future of Christian Ethics Committee Report," scethics.org/groups/2020-future-christian-ethics.
[28] The Society of Christian Ethics, "2020 Future of Christian Ethics Committee Report."

philosophy in the liberal arts core and majors that do not attract a large number of students.[29]

Awareness of the commodification of higher education implies that we cannot assume that our colleagues or students understand the importance of cultivating theological and ethical reasoning and its potential impact on the trajectory of higher education. We have to learn to speak across disciplines, including the language of business, in order to foster a more critical approach to employment policies within higher education. Theologians and ethicists too often rely upon the excuse that we have not been trained to think about budgets and to produce business models to project program sustainability. In my perspective, theology has always been about economics in terms of managing right relationships in God's household. Universities in the West first emerged from monastic communities where resources were shared in common. Moreover, economics and business in the past were taught in relation to disciplines such as moral philosophy, theology, and history. Revisiting more collaborative, cooperative, and conversational approaches to employment practices and university funding is essential and theologians and ethicists can influence a new trend.

Invite your department and other chairs to discuss and develop alternative models for funding universities.

Faculty members tend to raise issues of resource distribution as the main problem, but for smaller colleges and universities diminishing resources are also a problem. At the beginning of this essay, I emphasized the importance of context and significant differences in the financial circumstances and endowments of universities and colleges. Identifying new ways to fund universities and colleges and more ways to work collaboratively rather than in competition is a critical way chairs can help lead their institutions into a more just future and for the survival of the professoriate as a whole. In today's context, tenured chairs should educate ourselves and other fulltime faculty about our own economic position in relation to contingent faculty, specifically those who depend upon teaching to secure their livelihood. Chairs should research pluralist economics, cooperative economics, and steady state economics in order to design and suggest alternative and viable models for funding universities. A good example is the multi-stakeholder cooperative. Chairs in this way could contribute to and reframe business oriented and consumer driven models in education.

---

[29] One of the most well-known discussions of this was at Notre Dame University. See Heidi Schlumpf, "In Support of General Education that Includes Theology," *National Catholic Reporter*, August 15, 2015, www.ncronline.org/news/people/support-general-education-includes-theology.

Another option is to draw upon good work being done by universities who have changed their campus policies regarding contingent faculty by adopting multi-pronged strategies on their campuses. Villanova University, for example, adopted "multi-year contracts, clear governance representation throughout the university, and the beginning of conversations on paid leave to conduct scholarship."[30] Advocate for shared positions, multi-year contracts, the establishment of different ranks for adjunct faculty and, when arguing for tenure-track lines, consider flexible options such as shared positions with other departments. For example, a theological school or department of theology could encourage partnerships with programs at other institutions to begin roving theological schools where teaching responsibilities are shared and collaborative so that there are more fulltime positions that have full benefits.

Invite your department to articulate the ethic by which it aims to function and then continue to revisit that ethic when making decisions about relationships with contingent faculty.

As a theologian, values of fairness, reciprocity, collaboration, interdependence, accountability to a larger community, sustainability, and the inclusion of diverse peoples and experiences are the pulsating core of my work. These values should also be the core of our advocacy work within the university for justice, fairness, and pay equity for fulltime and part-time faculty. Bring these values to the center of the discussion in your department meetings and work together as a department to answer how you will embody them within your university. I publish biennially a theology department handbook. Such a publication could include statements about the department's understanding of inclusion of contingent faculty and values. Another possibility is to offer a course on university ethics either in the regular course schedule or through the faculty development office to create a vigorous and rich discussion of the changing nature of the professoriate and workers' rights as well as to accent the relationship of theology to economics.

Work across the university to change the campus narrative about contingent faculty.

There are many strategies one can use to accomplish this goal. Most importantly, consistently emphasize that the interests of fulltime tenured and tenure-track faculty and part-time faculty are interrelated. Specific strategies include challenging fulltime faculty when their

---

[30] The Delphi Project on the Changing Faculty and Student Success, "The Path to Change: How Campus Communities Worked to Change Non-Tenure-Track Policies and Practices," pullias.usc.edu/wp-content/uploads/2013/02/Villanova-University_PATH.pdf.

comments discount the intellectual vitality or creative contributions made by contingent faculty to university teaching. Sponsor dialogues on campus in the model of the Truth and Reconciliation Commission and the Church of Scotland's Poverty Truth Commission that bring administrators, board members, staff, and faculty together to across lines of difference to explore poverty and privilege within the university community as a whole.

Develop specific strategies to alleviate immediate needs of contingent faculty.

Contingent faculty may be reluctant to share immediate needs with chairs due to the precarious nature of their employment and fear of losing teaching opportunities. In order to address immediate needs, work with other chairs or a committee on contingent faculty concerns to create anonymous surveys of contingent faculty in order to better understand their working conditions at your university. You can also plan teaching schedules with justice and fairness in mind and that question past assumptions that the most senior and highest ranked faculty member should get priority scheduling. In addition, you can offer stipends for faculty to attend development events on a sliding scale by paying the highest paid faculty the least in order to encourage contingent faculty to take advantage of development opportunities. Or, chairs can help create a common purse on your campus where faculty and administrators can contribute development funds to provide more support for contingent faculty to remain active in their fields. Studies show that if adjunct faculty are supported in the ways that full-time faculty are supported the outcomes within the classroom, including the quality of their teaching, are the same.[31]

Advocate for the formation of unions at your institution.

Studies show that unions lead to better faculty working conditions for part-time faculty, including higher pay and benefits.[32] Better working conditions for fulltime and part-time faculty lead to better outcomes for students. Both part-time and fulltime faculties across the nation have organized with union groups such as the Service Employees International Union and United Auto Workers. A recent study done by the *Chronicle of Higher Education* on collective bargaining agreements made on 35 campuses showed that "unionized faculty

---

[31] Adrianna Kezar and Dan Maxey, "Faculty Matter: So Why Doesn't Everyone Think So?" *Thought and Action*, Fall 2014, www.nea.org/assets/docs/HE/e-Kezar.pdf.

[32] See Colleen Flaherty, "Union Raises for Adjuncts: As Unionization of Those Off the Tenure Track Spreads, There are Substantial Gains in Pay and Benefits," *Inside Higher Ed*, July 26, 2013, www.insidehighered.com/news/2013/07/26/adjunct-union-contracts-ensure-real-gains-including-better-pay.

have negotiated steady increases that are significantly higher, and some of the steepest gains have come from unions formed within the last few years."[33] Catholic universities and colleges have a special leadership role to play in creating just employment practices in higher education because one of the seven themes of Catholic Social Teaching is to promote the dignity of workers and provide for the right of workers to organize on behalf of their own well-being.

---

[33] Kristen Edwards and Kim Tolley, "Do Unions Help Adjuncts?" *The Chronicle of Higher Education*, June 3, 2018, www.chronicle.com/article/Do-Unions-Help-Adjuncts-/243566.

Toward an Inclusive Faculty Community

Matthew J. Gaudet

TO BE 'ADJUNCT' IS, BY DEFINITION, "Something joined or added to another thing but not essentially part of it."[1] Within the university context, there was a time when the title of "adjunct" professor was primarily descriptive of the role teaching played in the professor's life and career. Fifty years ago, "adjunct" faculty comprised about a third of the American professorate, but the vast majority of them were teaching either in addition to or in retirement from some other career. For these 'professors-of-practice,' professional experience in another career is what actually qualified them to teach in the first place.[2] Most of these instructors lacked a terminal degree but were instead hired to bring practical, professional experience (e.g. professional nurses teaching nursing practicums, successful entrepreneurs teaching business courses) that could balance the theoretical expertise of most scholars. That non-academic profession is also what allowed most of these adjunct instructors to teach without benefits and for relatively low pay since their primary career already provided for their livelihood.

Today, however, the qualifier "adjunct" more readily describes the relationship between the professor and the university community. In today's colleges and universities, 73 percent of faculty work off of the tenure-track, yet 73.3 percent of those indicate that they consider teaching in higher education their primary occupation.[3] That is to say,

---

[1] "Adjunct," Merriam-Webster Online Dictionary, www.merriam-webster.com/dictionary/adjunct?utm_campaign=sd&utm_medium=serp&utm_source=jsonld.

[2] Terminology for the subset of contingent professors who hold professional careers in another field is mixed and varies greatly from campus to campus, and often even between programs on the same campus. Lacking a universal standard, I have elected to follow the American Association of University Professors use of "Professor-of-Practice" (Ernst Benjamin, David A. Holinger, and Jonathan Knight, "Professors of Practice," *American Association of University Professors*, www.aaup.org/report/professors-practice.) It is worth noting that this usage of "Professor-of-Practice" differs from how James Keenan employed the term "Professor-of-the-Practice" in his opening essay in this volume.

[3] American Association of University Professors, "Data Snapshot: Contingent Faculty in US Higher Ed," www.aaup.org/news/data-snapshot-contingent-faculty-us-higher-ed#.W8T23FJRfMJ; The Coalition on the Academic Workforce, "A Portrait of Part-Time Faculty Members: A Summary of Findings on Part-Time Faculty Respondents

52 percent of college faculty today are neither on the tenure-line nor 'professors-of-practice' but adjunct *scholars*—with a terminal degree and research agenda—who have the misfortune to work off of the tenure-track.[4] These scholars occupy a liminal space in the contemporary university. On the one hand, by trade and self-identification, they are academics, but they lack the credentials, privileges, and pay of tenure-line professors. On the other hand, they are adjunct by title and rank, but they do not have the experience, professional stature, and the salary and benefits of a non-academic career to supplement their academic work. They exist in a university structure that was not constructed with them in mind, does not take them seriously, and, ultimately, offers them little more than the most tenuous and temporary of connections. Despite being the majority of faculty, they are literally "adjunct" to the institution.

The articles of this issue of the *Journal of Moral Theology* have thoughtfully and rigorously examined several distinct concerns that have arisen due to the adjunctification of Catholic higher education. Many of these issues involved justice for the adjunct professors themselves. However, when this issue is taken in total, one theme that seems to emerge is that this system has repercussions for the entire university or college. James Keenan, S.J., framed the issue of contingency on Catholic campuses as part of a larger void in university life: "The absence of a professional ethics at the university is evidence of and symptomatic of a university culture disinterested in ethics."[5] Kerry Danner and Debra Erickson showed that the ripples of mass contingency disturb the mission of Catholic higher education and the very notion of a Catholic university.[6] While this system is tragically

---

to the Coalition on the Academic Workforce Survey on Contingent Faculty Members and Instructors," www.academicworkforce.org/CAW_portrait_2012.pdf.

[4] A note on terminology: some scholars (and institutions) have begun to differentiate between the terms "adjunct" professors (who are typically part-time) and "contingent," "non-tenure-track," or "visiting" professors or lecturers (who are typically full-time). However, this terminology is far from universal. Moreover, while the distinction between full-time and part-time is meaningful, it is by no means the most meaningful way to parse the sets. Thus, I use the terms adjunct, contingent, and non-tenure-track (NTT) interchangeably. However, throughout this essay, I will maintain a linguistic distinction between adjunct/contingent/NTT *professors* (which is the entire set of faculty off of the tenure-track, inclusive of professors-of-practice) and adjunct/contingent/NTT *scholars* (which is the subset of NTT faculty who are not professors-of-practice, but trying to make their way primarily as scholars and teachers).

[5] Keenan, "University Ethics and Contingent Faculty," 8-25.

[6] Kerry Danner, "Saying No to an Economy That Kills: How Apathy Towards Contingent Faculty Undermines Mission and Exploits Vocation at Catholic Universities and Colleges," *Journal of Moral Theology* 8, special issue no. 1 (2019): 26-50; Debra Erickson, "Adjunct Unionization on Catholic Campuses: Solidarity, Theology, and Mission," *Journal of Moral Theology* 8, special issue no. 1 (2019): 51-74.

unjust for the contingent professor, Lincoln Rice, Karen Peterson-Iyer, Claire Bischoff, and Elizabeth Hinson-Hasty have shown several ways in which students and fellow faculty members also bear real costs in such a system.[7] All of this is to say, the issue of contingency is not just a justice issue, but a *community* issue, and, as such, it requires a communal solution.

In his opening essay, Keenan set the direction of this volume with a call to equity, solidarity, and community.[8] In this concluding essay, I will echo that call as I seek to address the problem of contingency from the perspective of the Christian community that our Catholic colleges and universities aspire to be. Jesus never offered us a sermon on the campus green, but it is still worth asking: what does Christ ask of our college communities? If we attend to this call, what might it mean for the non-tenure-track (NTT) faculty who have, thus far, been rendered adjunct to—that is, "added to but not essentially part of"—that community?

FACULTY ON THE MARGINS

The economic plight of contingent professors today is well documented. According to the American Association of University Professors, as of 2016, 73 percent of instructors in American higher education today work off the tenure-track.[9] Contingent contracts are certainly devoid of the protections of tenure but also typically lack the security and pay of permanent work.[10] The average pay per course is estimated at less than $3000, and the average annual pay for a contingent professor at a single institution was $20,506 in 2016.[11] Further exacerbating the problems is the fact that more than 50 percent of NTT

---

[7] Lincoln Rice, "The Threat to Academic Freedom and the Contingent Scholar," *Journal of Moral Theology* 8, special issue no. 1 (2019); Karen Peterson-Iyer, "Contingency, Gender, and the Academic Table," *Journal of Moral Theology* 8, special issue, no. 1 (2019); Claire Bischoff, "The Spiritual Crisis of Contingent Faculty," *Journal of Moral Theology* 8, special issue no. 1 (2019):92-114; Elizabeth Hinson-Hasty, "Department Chair as Faculty Advocate and Middle Manager," *Journal of Moral Theology* 8, special issue no. 1 (2019):126-140.
[8] James F. Keenan, *University Ethics: How Colleges Can Build and Benefit from a Culture of Ethics*(Lanham: Rowman & Littlefield, 2015), 54.
[9] American Association of University Professors, "Data Snapshot: Contingent Faculty in US Higher Ed."
[10] For a good argument for why tenure protections remain important even for those who do not research, see Rice, "The Threat to Academic Freedom and the Contingent Scholar" in this volume.
[11] American Association of University Professors, "Visualizing Change: Annual Report on the Economic Status of the Profession, 2016-17," www.aaup.org/sites/default/files/2015-16EconomicStatusReport.pdf.

faculty are relegated to part-time contracts.[12] These contracts typically lack any sort of health insurance, retirement savings, life insurance, funding for research or academic travel, or other benefits. Moreover, contingent contracts are often offered at the last minute—leaving precious little time to prepare—or, even worse, cancelled at the last minute with no remuneration for preparatory work already done. Finally, while some contingent professors do hold multi-year or at least yearly contracts, most commonly, contingent professors are hired and rehired every term or every year, typically subject to the unilateral decisions of the current department chair.

NTT professors deploy several methods for surviving in such conditions. Though relegated to "part-time" contracts, many scholars work at several schools (often totaling far more than a standard 40-hour "full-time" work-week but still without benefits). A 2014 congressional report suggested that as many as 89 percent of adjuncts work at more than one institution and 13 percent work at four or more schools.[13] The practice is so common that the literature has even coined a term—the "freeway flyer"—to refer to those who spend hours commuting between campuses, piecing together a living.[14] Other NTT scholars combine part-time teaching with other employment (in or out of academia). Others rely on the income and benefits of a partner or spouse for survival.[15] In some states, professors are eligible for unemployment insurance between semesters.[16] Finally, ac-

---

[12] American Association of University Professors, "Contingent Appointments and the Academic Profession," www.aaup.org/report/contingent-appointments-and-academic-profession.

[13] House Committee on Education and the Workforce Democratic Staff, "The Just-In-Time Professor: A Staff Report Summarizing eForum Responses on the Working Conditions of Contingent Faculty in Higher Education," democrats-edworkforce.house.gov/imo/media/doc/1.24.14-AdjunctEforumReport.pdf.

[14] Josh Boldt, "How I Got Out: One Adjunct's Journey From Freeway Flyer to e-Learning Director," *Chronicle Vitae*, chroniclevitae.com/news/575-how-i-got-out-one-adjunct-s-journey-from-freeway-flyer-to-e-learning-director; Mary Strope, "'Freeway Flyers' Now Make up the Bulk of Faculty," *Guild Freelancers*, www.guildfreelancers.org/news/2015/4/15/freeway-flyers-make-up-the-bulk-of-faculty.

[15] In "Contingency, Gender, and the Academic Table," Karen Peterson-Iyer has examined the gender implications of this kind of benefit reliance.

[16] In California in particular, the 1989 Cervisi vs. Unemployment Insurance Appeals Board decision established (fairly) that a promise or even a contract for the following semester is not a guarantee of future employment and thus, all contingent professors are eligible for unemployment insurance at the end of every term. J. Channell, Cervisi v. Unemployment Insurance Appeals Board, No. A038995 (Court of Appeals of California, First Appellate District, Division Four. February 1, 1989).

cording to a recent study by the UC Berkeley Center for Labor Research and Education, one in four families of part-time faculty are enrolled in at least one public assistance program.[17]

These realities have prompted a new genre of literature on academic contingency. While periodicals that focus on academic life (e.g. the *Chronicle of Higher Education*, *Vitae*, Insidehighered.com) took up this cause decades ago, it has more recently reached the mainstream news outlets, including *The Washington Post*, *The New York Times*, CNN, *Forbes*, *The Atlantic*, and *Salon*.[18] In 2016, the media news website Gawker.com even offered an 8-part series on contingent labor in academia.[19] Each of these sources tells a version of the same story: adjuncts are highly educated and often excellent educators, yet they are suffering from a nationwide epidemic of low wages, a lack of benefits, poor working conditions, short and sporadic contracts, and (to make ends meet) long commutes that often involve two, three, or even more institutions. Each source also vilifies the same antagonist—college administrators, whose pay and sheer numbers have increased exponentially over the same decades that have witnessed a massive shift from tenure-line to NTT faculty on campuses. Finally, each of these sources also offers the same solution: support unionization of contingent faculty and collective bargaining in order to increase pay and benefits.

One problem with this mainstream narrative is that it oversimplifies the issue into material terms and, consequently, material solutions. There is no doubt that the economic realities of contingent life are dire. However, like the tip of an iceberg, if we focus only on pay and benefits, we miss the far deeper social, emotional, and spiritual injustices

---

[17] Ken Jacobs, Ian Perry, and Jenifer MacGillvary, "The High Public Cost of Low Wages" *Berkeley Center for Labor Research and Education*, laborcenter.berkeley.edu/the-high-public-cost-of-low-wages/.

[18] Colman McCarthy, "Adjunct Professors Fight for Crumbs on Campus," *The Washington Post*, August 22, 2014, www.washingtonpost.com/opinions/adjunct-professors-fight-for-crumbs-on-campus/2014/08/22/ca92eb38-28b1-11e4-8593-da634b334390_story.html?utm_term=.9914046b3a9b; Corey Kilgannon, "Without Tenure or a Home," *New York Times*, March 27, 2014, www.nytimes.com/2014/03/30/nyregion/without-tenure-or-a-home.html; Gary Rhoades, "Adjunct Professors Are the New Working Poor," *CNN Wire*, September 24, 2013, www.cnn.com/2013/09/24/opinion/rhoades-adjunct-faculty/index.html; Dan Edmonds, "More Than Half of College Faculty Are Adjuncts: Should You Care?," *Forbes*, May 28, 2015, www.forbes.com/sites/noodleeducation/2015/05/28/more-than-half-of-college-faculty-are-adjuncts-should-you-care/; Laura McKenna, "The College President-to-Adjunct Pay Ratio," *The Atlantic*, September 24, 2015, www.theatlantic.com/education/archive/2015/09/income-inequality-in-higher-education-the-college-president-to-adjunct-pay-ratio/407029/.

[19] Hamilton Nolan, "The Educated Underclass," *Gawker*, gawker.com/tag/the-educated-underclass.

of the current contingent system.[20] For example, short and sporadic contracts certainly are the cause of financial hardship for contingent professors, but they also preclude the consistency around which a life can be planned and executed. Decisions like what neighborhood or town to live in or how to arrange for childcare are necessarily made with due consideration to where and when someone will be working. For contingent professors, however, such decisions are often not finalized until the last few weeks before a semester and, occasionally, even after a semester has already begun. Since courses get dropped from university schedules as a regular practice and for any number of reasons, NTT professors are often bumped out of their classes not only if *their* courses do not fill but also if a tenure-line faculty member needs a course. Since department chairs often make these decisions unilaterally, one's livelihood can be subject to staying in the good graces of one individual. Also, the short and fleeting nature of contingent contracts also makes it difficult to build relationships and become part of the campus community. This is especially problematic again for "freeway flyers," as no single campus may feel like home and the need to commute between multiple campuses means little time to develop the bonds of community even if one campus did rise above the others.

Many NTT professors are offered no office, no physical location to claim as their own, no place to store their belongings, and no place to meet with students. The irony is that they are still, somehow, required to hold "office" hours, typically in a coffee shop, cafeteria, or library on campus. Without an office, NTT faculty also typically lack a phone extension or voicemail, which often leads to them distributing their personal cell number to students. Finally, only rarely are NTT faculty issued computers. Instead they are usually left to purchase their own hardware, which may or may not integrate with the university's network, printers, and projection hardware. All of these policies combine to present the NTT professor as something "less than" a "real" professor to his or her students.

Similarly, contingent faculty are almost never given business cards or letterhead. Such costs are deemed by schools and departments as an unnecessary investment when the professor is only being hired by the semester. However, the lack of such tools prevents NTT faculty from presenting themselves professionally to publishers (for desk exam copies of textbooks, for example) and other professional colleagues. Likewise, on department websites, NTT faculty are often relegated to a list separate from the tenure line faculty, indicating that they are not only a rank below but really outside of the academic caste system altogether.

---

[20] See Claire Bishcoff's excellent "The Spiritual Crisis of Contingent Faculty" on contingency as a spiritual crisis in this volume.

Finally, NTT faculty are usually excluded from department meetings, faculty senate, and other committees where decisions on curriculum, policies, and standards get made, thus rendering 71 percent of faculty voiceless with regard to decisions that directly affect their work. Similarly, since it is wholly unheard of that an administrator would be hired directly from the contingent ranks, contingent faculty are further unrepresented when it comes to university decision-making. Even when NTT faculty unionize to gain a voice, typically their association is separate from and operates independently to the tenure-line union, which often pits the two labor organizations in de facto competition with each other.

In summary, while the economics of contingency are of vital importance and ought not be minimized, the issue cannot be dealt with in material terms alone. When one begins to consider the myriad of policies and practices that serve to alienate NTT faculty from the university community, it becomes clear that academic contingency is, in fact, a form of social and professional marginalization that goes well beyond, but is still intimately tied up with, economic and material deficiencies.

DEBUNKING THE MYTHS OF CONTINGENCY

Responding to contingent marginalization requires us to confront our understanding of what NTT faculty are and should be to the university community. As noted in the introduction, the contemporary contingency system was not planned for. It emerged from the classical professor-of-practice adjunct model, but little thought was given in the early years to how contingent scholars differ from professors-of-practice in both nature and needs. In the 1970s, the ratio of tenure line faculty to adjuncts was nearly inverted from what it is today (65 percent tenure line), and non-tenure-track faculty were almost always operating as professors-of-practice. Over the course of four decades, tenure line roles have given way to NTT roles at a steady rate, until today contingent scholars are the majority and tenure-line roles comprise only about a third of all faculty. The tepid pace at which this frog has been boiled has left a legacy in the form of three myths, which persist to keep non-tenure-track faculty on the margins of the university life. These myths must be debunked before we can proceed.

The Meritocracy Myth

It is commonly held that academia, for all of its politics, is idealized as a meritocracy. Those that publish well and often, teach well, and contribute their time and service to the university are supposed to gain tenure and rise through the ranks, while those who fail to meet these particular tasks do not. Scholars are also hired into their initial tenure-track positions based on merit or, more typically, potential for scholarly merit, as measured through a top academic pedigree and the recommendation of top scholars in the field. Ostensibly, then, academic rank (and the privileges that come with it) are the fruits of an individual's academic labor, and those who end up filling out the contingent ranks did not merit inclusion in the tenure-line ranks. This claim is worth exploring in greater detail.

Tenure is a credential that tends to be permanent and for life. Even when tenured professors change institutions, they tend to arrive at the new institution already tenured. At the same time, tenure is something that is achieved only once and at a single point in time. Thus, the fairness of the competition is highly subject to evolving market conditions. To put it more concretely, a scholar who was first offered a tenure-track job in 1975—when tenure-line faculty comprised 58 percent of the professional faculty on American college campuses—had a significant advantage in getting on the tenure-track compared to those who seek that same credential in today's market—when tenure-lines hover around 30 percent of all faculty. Using these numbers, even if all other working conditions remained the same, nearly half of those who are currently in contingent roles would have been hired on to the tenure-track in 1975.

All other employment conditions did not remain the same, however. The generational inequity has been further exacerbated by a significant increase in the number of doctorate holders on the market. From 1989 to 2007, the number of Ph.Ds. graduating and hitting the job market each year increased by 40 percent while the number of tenure-line roles in American colleges and universities only increased by 11 percent.[21] In short, as the demand for tenure-line jobs has reached an all-time low (as percentage of total professorate), the supply of candidates for those jobs has reached an all-time high.

Now, on the surface, the relatively low increase in tenure-line roles during these decades could of course be the result of a stagnating *need* for college professors. However, over the same period (1989-2007) in which tenure line roles increases by a mere 11 percent, total college graduates increased by a whopping 70 percent. Instead of filling this

---

[21] National Center for Education Statistics, "IPEDS Data Center," nces.ed.gov/ipeds/datacenter. Data compiled by the author. Note that while the total number of tenure-line roles did actually increase over the past four decades, this increase has not kept up with the corresponding increase in undergraduate and graduate students over those same years and has been dwarfed by the rapid rise in numbers of NTT professors over those same years. Since the *total* number of professors has increased relatively proportionately to students during these years, the most appropriate basis for comparison between generations is percentage of total professors that end up in tenure-line and NTT positions.

need with additional tenure-line roles, however, the steady trend between the mid 1970s and the mid 2000s has been the increasing use of NTT faculty. Making matters worse, while *full-time* contingent positions have ticked up slightly (13 percent in 1975 and 19 percent in 2014), the vast majority of newly created roles have been *part-time*. All of this begins to explain why a 2010 American Federation of Teachers study also found that 47 percent of part-time contingent faculty members would take a tenure-line role if it were available, but are trapped in a contingent role due to circumstance and market forces.[22]

The severity of these numbers begins to weaken meritocratic claims. First, when supply of doctorate-holders exceeds demand so greatly, short lists for openings include not one but several highly qualified candidates and ultimate hiring decisions are often made more on personal and academic fit than they are on merit.[23] Secondly, such an argument would have to reckon the inherent unfairness across generations. That is, if the threshold of entry to the tenure-line is significantly greater today than it was a generation ago, those who secured tenure-line jobs a generation ago did not earn them on merit alone but also on timing. Tenure itself only exacerbates this problem since a tenured professor who does not want to change jobs is largely protected from ever having to enter the job market again. This is not to say that the tenure system should be abolished.[24] It simply acknowledges that any claims to meritocracy are hollow when such protections are in place.

---

[22] "American Academic: A National Survey of Part-Time/Adjunct Faculty," *AFT Higher Education*, www.aft.org/sites/default/files/aa_partimefaculty0310.pdf.

[23] It is also worth acknowledging here that the same American Federation of Teachers report found that one third of contingent faculty have a preference for part-time work either because they already have a different primary occupation (24 percent) or because it allows them to devote time to family or personal matters (9 percent). The election toward family responsibilities, however, is one reason why the gender balance of contingent roles skews far more toward women than in the tenure-track ranks. See Karen Peterson-Iyer's "Contingency, Gender, and the Academic Table." on contingency and gender in this volume. Two points need to be made here about self-selection and scholarly merit. First, the decision to remain in a contingent role is not necessarily indicative of a less meritorious scholar. There is no reason to suggest that part-time status renders one a less effective teacher and, while part-time scholars may not publish as prolifically (since they necessarily do not spend as much time on the task, and they are universally not paid for the work), when they do publish there is no indication that their work is any less rigorous or scholarly than a tenure-line colleague. Secondly, it is important to distinguish between the choice to teach part-time and the socially constructed role that comes with that decision. Voluntary part-time professors are opting for fewer responsibilities, not second-class status or exclusion from the benefits of the tenure-track.

[24] See Lincoln Rice's "The Threat to Academic Freedom and the Contingent Scholar" in this issue on the moral imperative to expand, not restrict tenure.

Even excluding both of these points, however, an argument for meritocracy, quite simply, defies the facts. Ostensibly, a meritocratic system would make hiring decision based on a candidate's prospective ability to perform the central functions of a professor: teaching and research. Of these, the evidence on teaching is clear. Contingent faculty continually rise to the challenge and teach on par with or even above their tenure-line peers. A recent study from Northwestern University that showed "consistent evidence that students learn relatively more from non-tenure line professors in their introductory courses." Moreover, the study found that "differences are present across a wide variety of subject areas, and are particularly pronounced for Northwestern's average students and less-qualified students."[25] These numbers are particularly remarkable when considered against the significant handicaps that contingent faculty face every day.

Unfortunately, similar studies of *research* prowess among the contingent ranks are not available. Still, some conclusions can be inferred. First, since most initial tenure-track hiring decisions are made before scholars have really begun to make their scholarly mark, the decision is typically made on the prospect, not the reality, of merit, where the prospect of merit is measured with imprecise proxies such as graduating from a prestigious program or working with a prestigious scholar. A recent study in the *Chronicle of Higher Education* found that, for most disciplines, at least half of available assistant professorships went to candidates who were in their last year of Ph.D. studies, while 90 percent went to those within four years of completing their Ph.D. Furthermore, most of those who landed tenure-line jobs a few years after the doctorate held postdoctoral fellowships in the intervening years, not contingent positions.[26] In a true meritocracy, those who are further removed from their doctorate should have the advantages of more publications and more teaching experience when compared to freshly minted Ph.Ds. In reality, moving from contingent faculty to tenure-line has become an extremely rare event—meaning that those who, for any number of reasons, find themselves on the contingent side of the divide are extremely likely to stay there regardless of the work they do from that position.

---

[25] David N. Figlio, Morton O. Schapiro, and Kevin B. Soter, "Are Tenure-track Professors Better Teachers?," National Bureau of Economic Research, www.nber.org/papers/w19406. Introductory courses were used as the measure due to the study's methodology, which compared performance in later courses against the professor type students had in introductory courses.

[26] L. Maren Wood, "On the Academic Job Market, Does Patience Pay Off?," *The Chronicle of Higher Education*, October 16, 2015, www.chronicle.com/article/On-the-Academic-Job-Market/233683/.

Finally, even if we concede that contingent faculty publish less prolifically than their tenure-line colleagues, this would not prove the existence of a successful meritocracy. Rather, it would simply show that the advantages offered to tenure-line faculty have a very real effect on the amount of scholarship a scholar can produce. Even prior to tenure, junior professors on the tenure-track already possess an entire set of advantages over their contingent colleagues, including lower course loads, better pay, offices, travel funding, research funding, and research assistance. Many tenure-track junior professors even get course releases and sabbaticals with the express purpose of allowing them even more time to continue to publish. All the while, our so-called "part-time" faculty are working multiple jobs, commuting across several campuses, and teaching high course loads to make ends meet, leaving precious little time for research and publication. If a contingent faculty member is able to publish with even a fraction of the efficiency of her tenure-line colleague, it should be hailed as a remarkable accomplishment.

Yet, the opposite is true. In the academic hierarchy, almost invariably, contingent faculty are considered subordinate to even the greenest Assistant Professor. It does not matter if the contingent faculty member has several books published with high-ranking university presses or articles in all of the top journals. It does not matter if the contingent faculty member has been in the classroom for twenty years and has a remarkable and extensive teaching and service record. By rank, they remain at the bottom of the hierarchy and on the wrong side of the privilege divide.

In summary, the meritocratic justification of tenure-line privilege fails on several overlapping points. First, any claim to merit fails to account for the extreme differences in market conditions between generations. Second, even accounting for the market today, the severe oversupply of Ph.Ds. coupled with the decreasing supply of tenure-line roles typically leads to ultimate hiring decisions based more on luck and fit than on merit. Finally, those who—by bad luck or lack of fit—do not succeed in landing a tenure-line position directly out of graduate school immediately face severe disadvantages of time, funding, assistance, privilege, and prestige when compared to their tenure-track peers, creating a contingent vortex that is extremely difficult to escape. The meritocracy argument probably endures, in part, because there was a time when it was more or less true. Merit differences could explain the majority of those who did not end up on the tenure-track in the 1970s, when tenure-track was the norm, rather than the exception for graduating Ph.D.s and NTT roles aside from professors-of-practice were rare. Similarly, a later era in the history of contingency also gave rise to a second myth: that NTT roles can serve as a stepping stone to the tenure-track.

The "Stepping Stone" Myth

In the mid-1970s, the percentage of the professorate in contingent roles began to increase by a steady 1 percent per year. The effects of this steady shift in market prospects occurred in stages. At first, the shift was small enough that it was absorbed by the existing tiers. By the 1990s, however, tenure-track opportunities had been significantly displaced but were not yet outnumbered by part-time adjunct roles.[27] During this period, many of the new NTT positions were being filled temporarily by newly minted Ph.Ds. who did not initially find tenure-track jobs coming out of their doctorate programs. However, since tenure-track roles still outnumbered NTT scholars, there was still generally a viable route from contingency to the tenure-track. In fact, for many during this era, time as a NTT professor offered the nascent scholar a chance to gain some valuable teaching experience and begin a research agenda that would help to secure a permanent position.[28]

The existence of this period in academic history is likely why the stepping stone myth is so commonly told by senior scholars. For example, in her article in this issue, Kerry Danner noted that in her work with the American Academy of Religion's Academic Labor and Contingent Faculty Working Group she has "heard, more often than I would like to, department heads or administrators explain that adjunct teaching is a career stepping stone."[29] I would further suggest that those who offer such advice to NTT faculty are highly likely to have finished their Ph.D. in the 1990s or early 2000s and will often confirm that either they spent some time in a contingent position or knew others who had. Anecdotally, it would seem that the stepping stone path was indeed a viable one for a time.

The problem is the market today has shifted once again and the experience of those, now senior scholars, is no longer the norm. Today, contingent faculty outnumber tenure-line faculty by more than two to one, making it a statistical impossibility for contingency to serve as a reliable stepping stone to the tenure-track for more than a select few. Graduate programs are also graduating more Ph.Ds. than ever before, creating an oversupply problem that only exacerbates the

---

[27] The late 1980s was when total NTT positions first surpassed tenure-line roles in sheer numbers. However, when professors-of-practice are subtracted, tenure-line roles still outstripped NTT roles until the mid 2000s. See American Association of University Professors, "Contingent Appointments and the Academic Profession."

[28] American Association of University Professors, "Contingent Appointments and the Academic Profession."

[29] Danner, "Saying No to an Economy That Kills."

lack of demand. Furthermore, when at least half of available assistant professorships in recent years went to candidates who were in their last year of Ph.D. studies, and 90 percent went to those within four years of completing their Ph.D., and those who landed tenure-line jobs years after the doctorate held postdoctoral fellowships in the intervening years and not contingent positions, today the stepping stone myth is demonstrably false.[30]

Today's market is flooded with more Ph.Ds. that it can absorb, giving rise to two distinct professional tracks that emerge nearly immediately from the granting of the doctorate. And, as Keenan has neatly summed it up, "the gulf between tenured faculty and adjunct faculty has few secure ways of passage" across it.[31]

The Myth of Faculty Solidarity

Despite the gulf between tenure-line and NTT faculty, a notion of solidarity still exists between the two classes. This may be particularly true on campuses where faculty are unionized, where faculty unions are seen as fighting the same fight against the same antagonist, and there is strong encouragement from each class to support each other's negotiations with administration. However, it also emerges in interpersonal relationships on all campuses, where individual tenure-line faculty who recognize the injustice of contingency—a growing number today—offer sympathy and support for the struggle.

Yet, when those sympathies are tested, all too often they dissolve. In 2013, Robin Wilson offered the following report for the *Chronicle of Higher Education*:

> The first order of business when arts-and-science professors at New York University gather each year is to decide whether their full-time colleagues who work off the tenure track should be granted voting privileges in faculty meetings. This academic year, for the first time, the professors decided no. Extending the vote to full-time contingent faculty members was deemed too "dangerous." As on most campuses, professors at NYU who have tenure or are on the tenure track are a dwindling minority, and some worry that their power would be weakened and their voice muffled if shared governance were shared more broadly.[32]

This is stark example of what Keenan has termed the "cultural myopia" of tenure-line faculty. In short, "Tenure-line faculty probably,

---

[30] Wood, "On the Academic Job Market, Does Patience Pay Off?"
[31] Keenan, "University Ethics and Contingent Faculty."
[32] Robin Wilson, "The New Faculty Minority: Tenured Professors Retain Control as Their Numbers Shrink," *Chronicle of Higher Education*, March 18, 2013, chronicle.com/article/The-New-Faculty-Minority/137945/.

conveniently, do not care about adjuncts."[33] In this admission, he even includes his (former) self:

> In my ten years at my university, I have been working on faculty development, mentoring junior faculty, and developing programs for graduate students…. Still, in my university and in my department there are adjuncts. I know next to nothing about them…. I know little about the terms of their employment. Like other tenured faculty, I have unconsciously, and conveniently, worn blinders about their work context…. I have managed to tell myself they do not concern me.[34]

This myopia regarding academic contingency is supported by the three factors I have noted so far in this essay. First, in focusing on material inadequacies, the mainstream tale of contingency focuses on a single antagonist—the greedy administrator—rather than as a systemic and cultural problem. Under such a paradigm, tenure-line peers can express solidarity without much commitment beyond platitudes. After all, even department chairs have little power to change pay and benefits, and individual professors are completely powerless with regard to such material injustices.[35] However, if the mainstream narrative fails to account for social and structural marginalization of contingent faculty, as I have sought to show in this essay, then the problem is cultural, not hierarchical, and responsibility begins to fall on all who hold power and privilege in the community.

Second, holding on to the meritocracy myth also makes it easy to dismiss both the material deficiencies and the social marginalization of NTT faculty. When "publish or perish" is the mantra that drives pre-tenure scholars towards tenure, it becomes easy to regard NTT faculty as among those who have "perished" in a system that rewards academic merit. It ignores that initial hiring decisions—the point at which most end up in contingent roles—tend to be more of a function of timing, personal 'fit,' and 'potential' than they are about actual merit. It is blind to the privileges and advantages that come from getting hired on to the tenure-track, further stacking the deck and making the system far from meritocratic. However, if we blunt the power of meritocracy, then dismissing contingent faculty as somehow less worthy becomes far harder to excuse.

Finally, if contingency is understood as simply one more rung on the ladder toward tenure then the plight of contingency can be chalked up as "doing time" in order to earn the privileges that come with a

---

[33] Keenan, *University Ethics*, 40; Keenan, "University Ethics and Contingent Faculty."
[34] Keenan, *University Ethics*, 39–40; Keenan, "University Ethics and Contingent Faculty."
[35] Hinson-Hasty, "Department Chair as Faculty Advocate and Middle Manager."

tenure-track position. However, when NTT positions rarely function today as a "stepping stone" they promised a generation ago then the contingent faculty reality looks less like a rite of passage and more like systemic marginalization.

In summary, if we broaden the mainstream narrative on contingency and reject the trappings of the meritocracy and stepping stone myths, then the plight of contingency begins to be seen in a different light. Moreover, once we begin to accept that contingency is a form of social and structural marginalization, responding to the issue becomes the responsibility of faculty peers and not just administrative leadership. What remains, then, is to consider just what such a response might look like.

RESTORING THE CHRISTIAN COMMUNITY ON CAMPUS

There is little doubt that Catholic social thought (CST) would identify contingent professors as worthy of protection in the modern market driven university culture. Certainly, any response to contingency would have to begin with increasing pay and benefits. As stated in *Quadragesimo Anno* and elsewhere, justices requires workers to "be paid a wage sufficient to support him [sic] and his family" (no.71) and *Mater et Magistra* declares that "the remuneration of work is not something that can be left to the marketplace; nor should it be a decision left to the will of the more powerful" (no.71). However, the contingency crisis demands a deeper response. To this end, *Gaudium et Spes* expanded the claims above beyond mere material sufficiency: "remuneration for labor is to be such that man [sic] may be furnished the means to cultivate worthily his [sic] own material, social, cultural, and spiritual life and that of his dependents, in view of the function and productiveness of each one, the conditions of the factory or workshop, and the common good" (no. 67). *Laborem Exercens* stakes a right to shared governance: "Workers not only want fair pay, they also want to share in the responsibility and creativity of the very work process. They want to feel that they are working for themselves—an awareness that is smothered in a bureaucratic system where they only feel themselves to be 'cogs' in a huge machine moved from above" (no. 15). In short, while CST's emphasis on the protection of unions is often highlighted, a full reading of CST on worker justice reveals a driving narrative of the restoration of the *dignity* of the worker through the (re)establishment of dignified relations between the employer and the worker.[36]

---

[36] For a more extensive argument on contingency from the perspective of Catholic Social Thought, see Gerald J. Beyer, "Labor Unions, Adjuncts, and the Mission and Identity of Catholic Universities," *Horizons* 42, no. 1 (2015): 1–37, as well as Danner, "Saying No to an Economy That Kills" in this volume.

Even considering this, the direct calls to worker justice in Catholic social thought, helpful as they are, still cannot comprise a complete response to contingency on Catholic campuses. Catholic social thought also includes a firm commitment to the maintenance and expansion of community through an abiding attention to the common good and the solidarity of all of God's children. It is toward these themes that I am arguing Catholic higher education needs to fundamentally recommit itself. Pope Francis sums up the point well: "Here and now...the Lord's disciples are called to live as a community which is the salt of the earth and the light of the world. We are called to bear witness to a constantly new way of living together in fidelity to the Gospel. Let us not allow ourselves to be robbed of community!" (*Evangelii Gaudium,* no. 92) The gospel call to community is one of restoration and of radical inclusiveness. From the tax collectors Christ ate with to the prostitutes he socialized with, from the lepers he healed to the adulterer he protected and then forgave, so much of Christ's earthly ministry was aimed at restoring the communion between the communities he visited and those they had pushed to the margins.

Elsewhere, I have drawn upon the particular similitude between the plights of NTT faculty on campus today and the man born blind in in Chapter 9 of John's Gospel.[37] While the story is billed as a physical healing, that event is merely an incidental prelude. The main story examines how his community *reacted* to the healing and revealed the complex practices we employ in order to maintain our in-groups and out-groups and the status that comes with them. Blindness, at the time, was associated with sin, and this sin was understood as pretext for the exclusion of the blind man from the synagogue, the town, and even his own family unit. When Jesus and the disciples found him, he was literally on the margins of the town he was born in, begging for his food. When Jesus healed him, it should have restored his place in society. Instead, the pretext of disability and sin is revealed for what it was: an excuse to exclude and marginalize and thus reify one's own "proper" position in the society.

In today's university communities, we rarely exclude individuals on the basis of "sinfulness." However, we do rely on the myth of "merit" to form hierarchies and rank structures and exclude NTT faculty from the university community in dozens of ways. If my earlier argument against meritocracy holds then those who hold power and privilege in the university structure—especially administrators, department chairs, and tenure-line faculty—owe their contingent col-

---

[37] Matthew J. Gaudet, "Reflections on the Contingent Workforce at Catholic Colleges," in *Catholic Identity in Context: Vision and Formation for the Common Good* (San Francisco: University of San Francisco Press, 2018), 33–43.

leagues both an examination of personal conscience and an examination of the social structures that perpetuate the unjust power and privilege dynamics.

Such introspection is the necessary first step toward true Christian solidarity among all workers at Catholic colleges and universities. But it will not be easy. As Keenan observed, "Unlike most professionals and civil servants, we university faculty function very much as individuals in the academy. Aside from department meetings, we study alone, work alone, teach alone, write alone, and lecture alone; we also grade students individually and write our singular letters of recommendation."[38] Such siloing certainly enables the cultural myopia with respect to contingency. It also undercuts the real power of any claims to faculty solidarity. In the Catholic context, however, it is also antithetical to the common good. As Francis observes, "The radicalization of individualism in…anti-social terms leads to the conclusion that everyone has the 'right' to expand as far as his power allows, even at the expense of the exclusion and marginalization of the most vulnerable majority." Such radical individualism "denies the validity of the common good because on the one hand it supposes that the very idea of 'common' implies the constriction of at least some individuals, and the other that the notion of 'good' deprives freedom of its essence."[39] Thus, we observe cases of tenure-line faculty responding to the contingency crisis by circling the wagons and creating greater barriers to participation by contingent colleagues, despite ostensive claims to faculty solidarity.

Of course, any efforts to circling the wagons are antithetical not only to solidarity but to the common good as well. After all, as Rice has argued earlier in this volume, "If three-quarters of higher education faculty today are contingent, is it meaningful any longer to talk of academic freedom as a ruling principle in higher education?"[40] Or as Erickson has noted elsewhere, in the face of a changing academic landscape, perhaps "we are all contingent" more than we realize.[41] Recognizing that the present state of contingency foretells the future

---

[38] Keenan, *University Ethics*, 58.
[39] Francis, "Message from the Holy Father to the Participants in the Plenary Session of the Pontifical Academy of Social Sciences," April 28, 2017, https://press.vatican.va/content/salastampa/en/bollettino/pubblico/2017/04/28/170428h.html.
[40] Jan Clausen and Eva-Maria Swidler, "Academic Freedom From Below: Toward and Adjunct-Centered Struggle," *Journal of Academic Freedom* 4 (2013): 1-26, as quoted in Rice, "The Threat to Academic Freedom and the Contingent Scholar."
[41] Debra Erickson, "'We Are All Contingent': Advocacy and Solidarity in the Profession" Presented at Toward a Culture of University Ethics: An Interdisciplinary Conference, Boston, MA, 2017, www.bc.edu/centers/jesinst/toward-a-culture-of-university-ethics/speakers/day-three---wednesday.html.

of higher education as a whole offers important pretext for establishing universal faculty interdependence. For if the fate of NTT faculty is tied up with the fate of tenured faculty then tenured faculty need to make better efforts to support NTT faculty. Catholic notions of solidarity and common good, however, go even further than mere shared destiny and interdependence.

> Interdependence must be transformed into solidarity, based upon the principle that the goods of creation are meant for all. That which human industry produces through the processing of raw materials, with the contribution of work, must serve equally for the good of all (*Sollicitudo Rei Socialis*, no. 39).

Or, as interpreted by the US Bishops:

> We have to move from our devotion to independence, through an understanding of interdependence, to a commitment to human solidarity. That challenge must find its realization in the kind of community we build among us. Love implies concern for all… and a continued search for those social and economic structures that permit everyone to share in a community that is a part of a redeemed creation (*Economic Justice for All*, no. 365).

Catholic social thought does not allow for the picking and choosing of in-groups and out-groups based on ability, rank, or merit. Rather, Catholic notions of solidarity and the common good aim at a radically inclusive community where each of us—sighted or blind, tenured or not—is invited to the table. This is what Francis means when he pleads for us to "not be robbed of community." It is not some outside force that robs us of community but our own choices, and nowhere is this more true than the communities on Catholic campuses today. Locked in our silos, we rob ourselves of community. Sectioned by rank and status, we rob ourselves of community.

Keenan has called tenure-line faculty to "expand [the] circle of who deserves that meritorious title of 'colleague.'"[42] This is not merely a call to be friendlier to other individuals, but rather a call to recommitting the university to a "culture of ethics" and an "economy of life."[43] I would go even one step further and suggest that for all universities and colleges—but especially for Catholic schools which are committed to both Catholic social thought and the Catholic understanding of the mission and purpose of higher education—the culture of ethics ought to be oriented toward the common good, and we all

---

[42] Keenan, *University Ethics*, 54.
[43] Keenan, "University Ethics and Contingent Faculty"; Danner, "Saying No to an Economy That Kills."

must recommit ourselves to the kind of radical solidarity and inclusive community that Jesus offered us and invited us to extend likewise. 〖M〗

CONTRIBUTORS

Claire Bischoff teaches courses in theology and spirituality at St. Catherine University in St. Paul, Minnesota, where she is employed in a contingent capacity. She also serves as the theology professor for *Encuentro*, a summer theology institute for high school girls. She is co-editor of *Parenting as Spiritual Practice and Resource for Theology: Mothering Matters* (Palgrave, 2017) and *My Red Couch and Other Stories of Seeking a Feminist Faith* (Pilgrim, 2005). Mothering her three children, alongside teaching undergraduate and graduate students, is central to nurturing her sacramental imagination.

Kerry Danner is a part-time lecturer at Georgetown University, where she teaches courses on the virtues, social justice, and consumer culture as well as introductory theology classes. Her research interests are in character formation, economic justice, liberation theologies and the moral imagination, and her work has appeared in *The Journal of the Society of Christian Ethics* and *International Studies in Catholic Education* as well as various popular magazines. She currently serves as the American Academy of Religion's first Contingent Faculty Board representative and is actively involved in the Society of Christian Ethic's Caucus for Contingent Faculty Concerns.

Debra Erickson teaches ethics at Bloomsburg University. She received her PhD in religious ethics from the University of Chicago and researches and writes in the areas of university ethics, environmental ethics, global ethics, and ethics and politics. A co-founder of the Society of Christian Ethics' Caucus for Contingent Faculty Concerns, she is also co-editor of *Jean Bethke Elshtain: Politics, Ethics, and Society* (Notre Dame, 2018).

Matthew J. Gaudet is Lecturer of Engineering Ethics at Santa Clara University and is currently serving as co-chair of the Society of Christian Ethics Task Force on Contingency. His research lies at the intersection of Moral Theology and Political and Social Theory, with a particular interest in the topics of disability ethics, technology ethics, ethics of war and peace, and university ethics. His work has appeared previously in *The Journal of Moral Theology* and in *The Journal of the Society of Christian Ethics*, as well as popular periodicals such as *America* and *The National Catholic Reporter*.

Elizabeth Hinson-Hasty is professor of theology and currently serves at chair of the department of theology at Bellarmine University. Her most recent book, *The Problem of Wealth: A Christian Response to a*

Culture of Affluence (Orbis Books 2017), won a Catholic Press Association 2018 first place award for the best book related to Catholic social teaching. In addition, she has distinguished herself with an Award of Excellence for a Bible Resource from the Associated Church Press for *Reconciling Paul*, Horizons Bible Study (2015), as a Fulbright Scholar (Hungary 2010), with the Wilson Wyatt Faculty Fellowship for excellence in teaching and scholarship (2010), and a Kentuckiana Metroversity Award for Instructional Development for her course on Theology from the Margins (2008).

James F. Keenan, S.J., is the Canisius Chair and Director of the Jesuit Institute at Boston College. He is also the founder of Catholic Theological Ethics in the World Church (CTEWC) and co-chaired the international conferences in Padua, Trento, and Sarajevo as well as the regional ones in Nairobi, Berlin, Krakow, Bangalore, and Bogota. Today CTEWC is a network of over 1500 Catholic ethicists (www.catholicethics.com). Recently he wrote *University Ethics: How Colleges Can Build and Benefit from a Culture of Ethics* (Rowman and Littlefield, 2015) and edited, with Grant Gallicho, *Amoris Laetitia: A New Momentum for Moral Formation and Pastoral Practice* (Paulist Press, 2018). He is presently writing another book, *A Brief History of Catholic Ethics*.

Karen Peterson-Iyer, PhD, teaches ethics and theology in the Department of Religious Studies at Santa Clara University.

Lincoln R. Rice earned his PhD in moral theology at Marquette University in 2013. He has taught as an adjunct at both Marquette University and the University of Wisconsin-Milwaukee. In 2014, he published *Healing the Racial Divide* with Wipf & Stock. He is a member of the Casa Maria Catholic Worker community in Milwaukee and the Coordinator for the National War Tax Resistance Coordinating Committee.

STUDENT INTERNS

Patrick T. Fitzgerald, C'19 Mount St. Mary's University, is from Calverton, NY, and is earning a double major in Theology and Philosophy.

Sydney D. Johnson, C'19 Mount St. Mary's University, majoring in Philosophy with minors in History and Spanish, is from Lincoln, NE.

COVER ART

Sarah Hunter, a graduate of Saint Vincent College, Latrobe, PA, created "Fading Out," www.thecensoredartist.com.

Articles available to view
or download at:

https://msmary.edu/academics/schools-divisions/college-of-liberal-arts/journal-of-moral-theology.html

The

Journal of Moral Theology

is proudly sponsored by

The College of Liberal Arts
at
Mount St. Mary's University

www.ingramcontent.com/pod-product-compliance
Lightning Source LLC
Chambersburg PA
CBHW051939160426
43198CB00013B/2224